W9-CHK-863

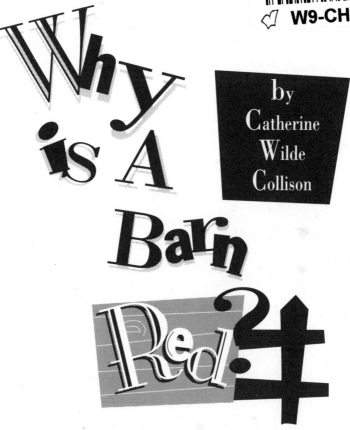

Why is A Barn Red?

by
Catherine
Wilde
Collison

the little book of BIG questions

Detroit Free Press

Credits

Cover design: Keith A. Webb
Illustrations: Keith A. Webb
Designer: Antoinette Cybulski Countryman
Copy editor: Patricia Foley
Contributors: Detroit Free Press staff writers
Back cover photo: Mary Schroeder

Published by the Detroit Free Press
Detroit, Michigan 48231

ISBN 0-937247-58-8

Introduction

Young readers have a natural curiosity about the world around them. They get to the heart of the matter with their questions, and they ask things adults usually can't answer off the top of their heads — questions such as "Why is a barn red?" and "How do they change the lights on the Mackinac Bridge?" and "What was the most unusual pet in the White House?"

This book came to be because of those questions, just a few of the hundreds young readers have asked the Detroit Free Press' News for Young Readers column. It includes many of the relatively timeless questions we've received as well as those reflecting the changing news.

The column began during the Persian Gulf War, when this paper's editors decided young readers needed a place for straight answers.

When the war ended, the questions continued — on people, places and events around the world. It's been my happy task to write or edit answers for the many young readers who call or write the Free Press. They're the true assignment editors — and pretty challenging ones.

The job has been made easier by fellow Free Press experts, who are on call to answer questions. You'll see the reporters' names with some of the answers they contributed. You'll see the names of other experts who helped at the back of the book. None of the questions was easy to answer, but we always found people willing to tackle them, especially when they knew a young reader was asking.

– Catherine Wilde Collison

This book is dedicated
to all young readers with questions.

Contents

? Bugs, beasts and birds

Will killer bees ever come to Michigan?

Chris Miller, Lake Orion

No, it's too cold for killer bees here.

Killer bees, really called Africanized honeybees, got their nickname after reports that they killed animals and people with their stings. It's not that their stings are worse than the stings of regular honeybees. Killer bees just fight harder to defend their nests. Animals have been killed when they couldn't run away; people have been killed when they got too close to a nest and couldn't get away fast enough.

1

Since mayflies (fish flies) live only a short time, where do they come from? Do they migrate?

Adam Litle, Grosse Pointe Park

Mayflies come from ponds, lakes or streams, usually ones that have clean and clear water. In Michigan, that can be anywhere in the state; but they are weak flyers, so they don't migrate or move far from where they are born.

The time they live varies. Some adult mayflies, such as the ones you probably saw near your home in Grosse Pointe Park, live only about 48 hours. Other adult mayflies live as long as four to six weeks.

That's only the adult life, though. Mayflies actually have a total lifetime of a year. During the winter, the young mayflies, which are called naiads, have no wings and live in the lakes and ponds, eating such things as dried leaves and dead insects.

In the spring, they get wings, but they are not considered full-grown because they cannot reproduce.

By summer, they are old enough to be adults and produce a new family of mayflies.

How can bugs tell each other apart?

Julia McMath, Detroit

Most bugs don't really recognize other bugs. They don't have the ability to tell the difference, for example, between a bee and a beetle.

Insects can recognize their own kind, though. Bugs use vision, smell and sometimes sound to do this.

For example, a cricket would recognize another cricket by its chirping sound. A firefly can tell another firefly by the flashing light it gives off, which acts like a signal.

Some insects that eat other insects have a little more ability to find other bugs. The dragonfly, which feeds off smaller bugs, has very large eyes and can see long distances to help it find prey. Many other bugs can see less than a few inches around them, so they wouldn't notice other insects.

Why do lions kill cheetahs if they are both in the same family and of the same land?

Gary Bell, Detroit

Being in the same family — the feline family — doesn't stop the lions and the cheetahs from killing each other. Both kinds of animals live in the same parts of Africa, usually in grassy areas near forests and water.

Lions kill cheetahs because they are competing with them for food, such as the zebra and antelope, in the same land. The lion is stronger, so it can kill the cheetah, even though the cheetah is faster.

Sometimes lions eat young cheetahs because they are especially easy to catch. The lion, like other animals, puts survival first. If there is too little food to share, the lion will kill animals that take the food and also will kill weaker animals for a meal. A lion will even kill another lion, if two male lions are competing to lead a lion family.

Why are animals being used for medical tests?

Nick Panza, Shelby Township

Scientists need to know how a body will respond to new drugs or medical procedures. They sometimes use animals instead of people in their tests to make sure that people won't be hurt if the new drug or medical procedure doesn't work.

The animals' bodies are like human bodies in many ways. By looking at how a test affects an animal, scientists can sometimes tell how the test would affect a person. For example, at the University of Michigan, rats have been used in a test that may help relieve high blood pressure, which can lead to heart attacks.

In another test, the hearing of a live guinea pig has been tested in research to develop an artificial ear for humans.

In some cases, the scientists have to remove and study a part of the animal's body after the test. That's another reason they use animals instead of people for the tests.

How can I save the manatee?

Julielyn Gibbons, South Lyon

First, there are many things to learn about these freshwater mammals that can grow to the size of elephants.

There are several kinds of manatees. The kind that's best known in this country lives in Florida's fresh waters and in the shallow edges of the oceans. In the summertime, some of the snub-nosed beasts swim as far north as Georgia.

There are about 2,000 of these manatees left. There used to be many more, but the manatees are dying fast as people build homes near rivers and canals.

In 1992, 140 of them died in Florida. Manatees normally live about 45 years, eating only sea grass and other plants.

The best thing to do to help manatees is to keep their environment clean.

Many hurt manatees are taken to Sea World in Orlando, where they grow strong and are set free again.

By Emilia Askari

Does spring weather affect animals at the zoo? Do they get sicker?

Erika Glenn, Detroit

Yes, spring weather does affect the animals, and more animals in the zoo get sick in the spring than at any other time.

There are several reasons:

■ Animals are under stress because they have been living all winter in spaces that are smaller than their outside spaces and less like the way they live in nature.

■ Animals haven't had as much exercise indoors, so their bodies are weaker.

■ Changes in the weather — from warm spells when animals go outside to snows when animals go back inside — make them less able to fight off colds and germs.

Spring is also a time when zoos bring in new animals or ship their animals to other zoos. Traveling is stressful for the animals; they may arrive tired and may get sick. New animals are kept in the zoo's hospital for more than a month to make sure they are not bringing germs that would spread to other animals in the zoo.

What do zookeepers do with the animals in winter?

Danielle Canterbury, Taylor

Animals don't leave the Detroit Zoo in Royal Oak, but those that like warmer climates stay indoors more.

Mainly, zookeepers have to supervise all the animals more than in warm periods — checking on their diet and exercise and making sure they don't get bored.

Here are some examples of what happens:

■ The elephants are taken for walks indoors, doing regular laps around their rooms.

■ The chimps and other primates are given play times with balls and other toys so they won't feel too cooped up.

■ Parts of the outdoor areas are shoveled and cleared for the polar bears. They stay outside a lot.

■ Most animals have more food in the winter. The sea lions, who eat about 18 pounds of fish a day in the summer, get almost 30 pounds a day in the winter.

■ The oryx has a fragile horn that can break when it's cold, so the animal is let outdoors only for short times.

I would like to know why animals hibernate. Why don't they just eat all they want and survive the winter?

Anne Mitchell, Novi

Some animals hibernate because that's the best way for their bodies to work in the winter. Hibernation means the body system slows down and the temperature inside an animal's body drops to near freezing.

When days get shorter — meaning there are fewer hours of daylight — it signals that winter's coming, and it signals the animal's body to change.

Animals that hibernate build up fat from eating a lot before they hibernate. In Michigan, for example, the woodchuck hibernates. It eats nuts and plants as well as flowers, which are not available in the winter.

Other animals, by the way, have different ways of adapting to the winter. Some, such as birds, go south.

9

What is the most endangered animal around our area?

Amy Coon, Lapeer

The lynx (LINKS) is the most endangered in Michigan. Lynxes live in the Upper Peninsula.

The other Michigan mammals on the endangered species list are the gray wolf, the cougar and the Indiana bat.

Michigan sets its own rules on what animals, fish, plants and insects are endangered.

If an animal is on the state endangered list, there are fewer than 100 left in Michigan, or there are three or fewer places where that species exists.

What kinds of animals are endangered?

Danielle Brett, Lapeer

All kinds.

An animal that lives in a unique habitat, which is the home that provides food, shelter and plants, is most likely to be among the endangered animals.

If that habitat is destroyed and the animal can't travel or live anywhere else, it would be at risk. Many animals cannot live in cities or near people. If a woods or grassy area is built over, those animals don't have homes.

Animals are also threatened when people want to collect parts of their bodies, or the animals, birds or insects themselves.

Here is what the World Wildlife Fund, which checks the health and safety of wildlife, believes are the 10 creatures most in trouble because humans are trying to collect or hunt them:

ANIMAL	WHERE
Siberian tiger	Mainly in Russia and China
Black rhino	Africa
Orangutan	Sumatra and Borneo
Moluccan cockatoo	Indonesia
Giant panda	China wilderness
Asiatic black bear	Asia
Hawksbill sea turtle	Tropical ocean reefs
Bog turtle	Eastern United States
Orinoco crocodile	Venezuela
Bird-wing butterfly	Around the world

What is the most endangered species in the world?

Sara Bowersock, Utica

A species refers to one unique type of creature. The Spix macaw is the most endangered. In 1993, there was only one pair of Spix macaws left, in a jungle in northeast Brazil.

How many birds are on Earth?

Theresa Maraatz, Detroit

About 50 billion. That's about 10 times as many birds as people on Earth, and 200 times as many birds as people in the United States.

Of course, people can't count every bird; but they do count some birds and estimate based on how many they see.

Why do birds sing in the morning?

Beverly Greenwood, Detroit

There are several reasons.

For one, birds sing to mark their territory — the area a bird considers its property. That could be several backyards for a robin, for example.

In spring, you hear a lot of singing in the morning, because that's the time of day many new birds arrive from more southern areas seeking a northern home.

The birds who already have arrived are singing to signal

that the yards or trees are occupied.

Many birds sing as a way to show off their health. A sick bird wouldn't sing in the morning — and a bird that wanted to take over its area could try to move in if it didn't hear singing.

Another reason birds sing in the early morning is that it's too dark for them to do other things, such as find food.

Though birds sing at other times of the day, you often notice the sound more in early morning, because there is not much wind. Sounds carry better then.

In Michigan, you probably hear a lot of cardinals and robins singing in the morning.

I have been watching the birds fly north. Why do they fly in a "V" formation?

Sean Peter Battiste, Boyne City

Groups of large birds such as Canada geese fly in the shape of a "V" because it saves the birds energy.

The V-formation allows each bird to see what's ahead, but at the same time it uses the updraft or swirling wind in the air created from the flapping wings of the bird in front. A bird gets to rest its inner wingtip on the rising wind from the bird in front.

Of course, the lead bird doesn't have this help, so the geese take turns being in the lead.

Sports

What was the highest score in baseball history?

Eric Black, West Bloomfield Township

The highest score in baseball history was Chicago Cubs 26, Philadelphia Phillies 23, on Aug. 25, 1922. That was in a National League game. The highest score in American League history was Boston Red Sox 22, Philadelphia Athletics 14, on June 29, 1950.

By the Free Press sports staff

Why do they play "The Star-Spangled Banner" at sporting events?

Brooke Ternes, Grosse Pointe Farms

There's no one reason why people play "The Star-Spangled Banner" before many sporting events, but it has become a tradition. The custom is usually dated to early baseball games. "The Star-Spangled Banner" wasn't named the national anthem until 1916. As far back as 1917, "The Star-Spangled Banner" was played at several games in major league parks; but it was usually only on special occasions such as opening day and World Series games, when bands were hired.

"The Star-Spangled Banner" was played, for example, when the New York Giants went up against the Chicago White Sox in the 1917 World Series. It wasn't until after World War II that it became more common. It's not a rule in most places.

One place where it is a rule is in the Big 10 Conference; U-M, MSU and all the other Big 10 schools must play the national anthem before major sports events such as football games.

In the movie "A League of Their Own," Madonna makes a catch with her cap. If a Detroit Tiger made the same catch with his cap, as opposed to his mitt, would it be considered a legitimate catch?

Tyler Graves, Mt. Clemens

No. That's against the rules.

The major league rule book says that for a catch to count, it must fit this definition: A fielder must catch the moving ball in his hand or glove and be firmly holding it — providing he does not use his cap, protector, pocket or any other part of his uniform in getting possession.

By John Lowe

On Tiger games that are televised, on the wall it says: "No Pepper Games." What does that mean?

Mark Adams, Canton

A pepper game is more of a fun drill than a game. A batter using bunts and half swings hits the ball to several players who stand, usually side by side, much closer to the batter than in a game. Whichever player catches the ball pitches it back to the batter. No one wins or loses.

Players need quick reflexes for a pepper game, because many of the balls are line drives. This drill also helps improve fielding skills and coordination.

At Tiger Stadium, the signs about no pepper games are rules for home and visiting teams to follow. The words are written on the stadium wall at several places where the drill would be dangerous if a ball went into the stands. Fans who come to games early wouldn't be watching out for the ball as they do during a regular game.

Teams can play pepper games in some areas of the stadium, such as behind home plate, where a screen or netting would keep the ball from hitting fans.

There's no set schedule for the drills; they're not routine for the Tigers.

By Free Press staff

In Wimbledon tennis — how do they pick the first matches?

Jimmy Heron, Northville

Players are matched based on a combination of their ranking, or seed, and a random drawing. The seed is determined by how well the player has performed in tournaments in the past year.

At Wimbledon and other tennis tournaments, the goal in organizing the matches is not to have the top players play each other too early in the tournament.

To do that at Wimbledon, a long sheet with 128 lines is set up for the 128 players. The top 16 players are placed in slots that keep them farthest apart. Those slots are positions 1, 16, 17, 32, 33, 48, 49, 64, 65, 80, 81, 96, 97, 112, 113 and 128. Position No. 1 automatically goes to the No. 1 player; position 128 to the No. 2 player.

Among the remaining 16 top players, there is a drawing to see whether they are in the top half (above 64) or the bottom half of the assigned positions that keep the players spread out.

What is pelota?

Brad Obie, Highland

Pelota (pay-LOW-tah) is a type of handball that became popular in parts of Spain and France more than 600 years ago. The sport spread to South American countries, as well as Mexico and Cuba.

There are several types of pelota. All types have the goal of hitting a ball against a wall so that the opponent cannot return it before it bounces twice.

Some games are played barehanded with leather balls. Others are played with hard rubber balls and two-member teams using basket-like gloves strapped to the wrists to toss the ball.

A type of pelota called jai alai (HIGH-ligh) is played professionally in Florida.

How come the Detroit Pistons do not have a cheerleading team?

Tracey Howard, Detroit

The Pistons don't have a cheerleading team because the Pistons management doesn't think they need one.

The Pistons did try to draw crowds earlier with a dance and cheerleading troupe called the Classy Chassis. It gave its last hurrah in 1984.

People managing the Pistons say:

■ Cheerleading is an old idea. Basket-shooting contests, electronic ball races and video clips have taken its place.

■ Companies that used to sponsor cheerleaders now prefer the new kinds of entertainment.

■ The Palace, where the Pistons play their home games, doesn't have a good place for cheerleaders to stand.

Pistons fans have not always liked having cheerleaders.

But the Pistons still like to hear cheers. So they sometimes display a volume meter — a needle-like device that moves as the sound of fans' voices gets louder. Pistons management wants fans to encourage other fans to cheer.

What is the Stanley Cup named after and how much is it worth?

Greg Pilarski, Sterling Heights

The Stanley Cup, the trophy given to the National Hockey League champion, was named after Lord Stanley of Britain, who gave it to Canada in 1893.

Lord Stanley was governor-general of Canada; he represented Britain's Queen Victoria. Canada was part of the British empire.

He loved hockey, which his sons played. He wanted to leave a gift to Canada before he went back to Britain. The cup was given first to amateur hockey champions; in 1910 it became the property of the National Hockey Association and now belongs to the National Hockey League.

The top part of the trophy, the original cup, is kept in the Hockey Hall of Fame in Toronto. Another cup is used now. Its base gets bigger as rings are added. The rings are where the names of winning teams' members are engraved.

No one knows for sure how much it's worth.

How come the announcers in TV's professional sports use such odd expressions as "the ball bounced off the iron" instead of "off the rim"?

Brian King, St. Clair Shores

The sports announcers are just trying to keep things interesting. Instead of using the same words over and over, they try using different words to tell what's going on in the game. They also try to paint a clear and colorful picture of the game. So instead of saying somebody "jumped up for the ball," they might say the player "took to the sky."

The terms are often invented on the spot, right in the middle of the action.

George Blaha, who has announced Detroit Pistons games for many years, says he uses special terms because people who play professional basketball have special talents.

Why do we have the Olympics?

Tara Johnson, Livonia

The world has the Olympics now mainly because of the efforts of a Frenchman about 100 years ago.

Baron Pierre de Coubertin decided he wanted to restart the games begun by the Greek people who honored their gods with athletic contests more than 2,700 years ago. Because these games meant stopping any wars while athletes competed, the games became symbols of peace and unity.

The first modern Olympic games took place in 1896.

But the modern games did not always stop wars. In fact, sometimes wars stopped the games: The games were called off in 1916 because of World War I and again in 1940 and 1944 during World War II.

The goals of the International Olympic Committee, which runs the events and sets the rules, are:
■ To make friendships among all countries stronger.
■ To encourage sports development and sports contests around the world.

Why did ancient Greeks run naked in the Olympic games?

Michael Povv, Russia, of the Children's International Summer Village in Wixom

When was the first Olympics?

Erin Shozlin, Bloomfield Hills

The main reason Greeks competed nude was a practical one: Their robe-like clothing would slow them down or limit movement.

The climate was warm, so competing without clothing was not a problem. Women were banned from competing or watching. The male athletes didn't mind showing their bodies and the spectators didn't mind seeing them. The art and culture of the time often showed naked bodies.

The early Olympics were more than 2,700 years ago as part of a festival honoring the gods in Olympia. The first recorded Olympics in 776 B.C. ("B.C." stands for "before Christ") included events such as foot races and wrestling.

Spectators showed approval for an athlete by snorting and smacking their lips.

How do people get in the Olympics?

Rachael Garfinkle, West Bloomfield Township

Each international sports federation, or group, sets its own rules on how athletes qualify to compete in the Olympics. The International Track and Field Federation, for example, decides what it takes to qualify for the Olympics in that sport.

Usually, top athletes compete in local and regional

tournaments, then move on to national and world tournaments before they qualify for the Olympics.

There is one general rule: Active athletes must be part of the group that sets up the requirements.

For more information, write the sport in which you are interested, and send a letter to:

United States Olympic Committee
1750 East Boulder St.
Colorado Springs, Colo. 80909

Is the torch used in the Winter Olympics the same torch used in the Summer Olympics?

Sarah Pritchard, Romeo

No.

Each Olympic Games has its own torches.

For the Summer Games in Barcelona, Spain, in 1992 each runner had his or her own torch to carry in the relay run to Barcelona.

When one runner finished his or her part of the run, that runner lit the next runner's torch. They passed on the flame by lighting the next torch, but not by passing the torch itself. The last runner lit the torch at Barcelona for the opening ceremonies.

The first runner to carry the torch on the 50-day trip from Olympus, Greece, to Barcelona had his torch stolen. He had lit the next runner's torch and was walking back to Olympus when a man asked to carry it. That man stole it.

The torches are made of aluminum and designed to keep the flame burning through chemicals inside. They are worth at least $150. The runners get to keep their torches as souvenirs.

What do the Olympic rings stand for?

Michael Sandmark, Southfield

The five interlocking rings on a white background stand for the five parts of the world that had countries competing in the 1920 Olympics. They were:

- Europe.
- Asia.
- Africa.
- Oceania (Australia and the islands around it).
- North America. (Countries from South America did not compete then.)

The flag was designed in 1914 for use in the 1916 Olympics, but the games were called off that year because of World War I.

Nowadays, the ring for North America symbolizes both South and North America.

The symbols are used around the world to stand for the international games.

If you cashed in Olympic medals, how much would they be worth?

Michael Berry, Livonia

There's no set price. They are worth as much as collectors are willing to pay.

Older medals usually sell for more. One of the highest prices paid for a medal was $9,350 in January 1992 for a gold medal from the 1932 Winter Olympics in Lake Placid, New York.

Most medals just show the year and the place.

Athletes who sell their medals often are embarrassed and don't want their names known. So a buyer usually doesn't know whose medal it was.

Buying medals usually is done by mail through special dealers because collectors may live anywhere in the world.

Americans are the biggest collectors.

Were the gold medals in the Barcelona Olympics hollow? I'm also curious whether the silver and bronze were the same.

Jerry Burkett, Ferndale

None of the medals were hollow. The first-place medals (675 of them) at the 1992 Summer Olympics in Barcelona, Spain, had a silver base, which was covered in gold. They were designed by a Spanish sculptor and had a modern design on them to represent the city of Barcelona. The silver medals were all silver, but the bronze medals had some copper in them. The medals were almost 3 inches wide. The gold ones weighed about half a pound.

In the Summer Olympics, they have professional sports players playing. How come professional players in the NHL can't play in winter?

Simone Sanders, Detroit

A professional player from the National Hockey League can play in the Winter Olympics — but only if his team agrees to let him.

Because the Winter Olympics are held during the hockey season, most teams don't want to let valuable players miss games.

Michigan

Where does the water go when it goes out of the Soo Locks?

Tom Basco, Grosse Pointe Park

Practically all the water goes back out into the St. Marys River.

The water in the river, which is coming from Lake Superior, is divided three ways as it flows toward Lake Huron: into the locks, into power stations and through the St. Marys rapids.

The locks, which are used to help ships pass from the higher Lake Superior water level to the lower level in Lake Huron, close for the winter by Jan. 15 or earlier, depending on the weather.

But you can't see any difference in Lake Huron. Only 1 percent of the water flowing from Lake Superior is used to run the locks. A small amount of water stays in the locks while they are closed.

The locks open in March.

What are those "Adopt-a-Highway" signs for?

Sandhya Krishnan, Bloomfield Hills

Those signs mark where volunteers have promised to help pick up litter from a section of roadway.

Companies, community groups or individuals who adopt a highway promise to pick up litter for two years, at least four times a year, on a stretch of road.

In Michigan, 3,400 miles of roadway — that would be farther than the distance from Detroit to Los Angeles — are adopted.

Some roadways, such as I-696 with its high walls, can't be adopted because they're dangerous and hard to clean.

The state picks up litter, too, but state workers say the volunteers help them by reaching areas farther back from the road.

It's against the law to litter, but people do it anyway. Summer is a big litter time, with more people driving.

WANT TO HELP? **To adopt a highway, you can write:**
Office of Communications, MDOT,
PO Box 30050, Lansing 48909.

How many gallons of paint does the state of Michigan use a year on roads?

Michelle Bissell, Lakeview

About 445,000 gallons of paint are used every year to paint state roads, which is done between May 1 and Oct. 1. The roads

28

include interstate freeways such as I-75. The state does not paint county or city streets.

Every year, the state repaints all the lines that separate traffic because those lines get worn off by winter weather, road salt and snowplows.

The state uses 130,000 gallons of white paint and 315,000 gallons of yellow paint. That's enough to put lines on 10,000 miles of road.

This paint is a mixture that contains ground-up glass beads. They are supposed to help the lines show up better by reflecting vehicle lights.

Where did Detroit's Indian Village get its name?

Erin Deane, Detroit

The name was given to the area by the people who owned the land that became the east side Detroit neighborhood. The owners picked the name in 1895, when they were selling the land that would be subdivided into lots for houses.

There was no direct historic connection to American Indians when they named it. The land was a farm before it was sold. Probably Indians lived there at one time years before that, since some Indian artifacts have been found nearby, as well as relics of the British military units that later came to Detroit.

How do they change the lights on the Mackinac Bridge?

Phillip Hughes, Flushing

The lights are changed in the same way you change a light bulb in your own house, by unscrewing the bulb and putting a new one in. But of course, it's very hard to get to where the lights are.

On the Mackinac Bridge, there are 98 lamps, each about 300 feet apart, on the bridge's cable wires.

About a dozen lights need changing a year.

First, a worker takes an elevator inside a bridge tower up to the main cable on the bridge. Each side has a main cable that is about 2 feet thick. Walking along the cable is like walking on a round pipe. The worker holds onto smaller cables near that main cable and has a safety belt attached to one of the smaller cables.

When the worker gets to the light, the colored cover (red, green or amber, which is a shade of orange) is unscrewed.

The worker then changes the bulb and screws the colored cover back on.

Besides the colored lights on the cables, there are other safety lights along the roadway on the bridge.

Fall used to be a time when all the colored covers in the cable lights were changed because only amber covers were used in the summer. But people said they liked the different colors, so since 1988, the multicolored ones have been used year-round.

? The changing world

In the past, were South America and Africa joined together?

Bethany Murray, Taylor

Yes. The two continents were one mass of land more than 130 million years ago.

There was a rift, or crack, in the land. Along this crack, the earth began to break apart into two sides 125 million years ago. As the crack widened, waters from the sea entered.

This happened very slowly. The crack widened at about the same pace that fingernails grow — about an inch a year.

31

How high up in the mountain was the iceman found in 1991? If people climbed there, why didn't they find him earlier?

Jamie Wallace and Brendan Neall, Birmingham

The body, believed to be at least 4,000 years old, was found in September of 1991 in Austria 10,500 feet high on a mountain glacier in the Alps. (That's higher than 10 of RenCen's center towers stacked one on top of another.)

The body wasn't found earlier because the glacier was larger and covered it with ice.

Because this body was under ice out of the sunlight, it didn't melt during a warm spell 700 years ago.

Why did the iceman found in 1991 have straw shoes and not leather shoes? Why did he have a stone ax in his hand?

Melanie Harrison, Rockford

The ax found with the body discovered in the Austrian glacier had a bronze blade, but a stone knife or arrowhead was also found with the man. His shoes weren't made of straw; they seem to have been leather shoes stuffed with straw for extra warmth.

He was probably carrying the tools to hunt or protect himself. People at that time and in that area did have homes and did farm. This man could have been traveling to another village since he also was carrying a backpack. People who lived 4,000 years ago, during a time called the Bronze Age, began to make tools of metal, instead of just stone. They also knew how to make clothing and shoes of leather from animal skins.

Who are the Kurds and where are they from?

Melissa Mitchell, Livonia

The Kurds are a group of people who live in an area of western Asia called Kurdistan (KUR-dih-STAN), or Land of the Kurds. Kurdistan is not a country. It is a region that is part of several countries. It is a land of high mountains with some low areas near the Tigris River. Kurdistan is a little smaller than Michigan.

People started going to Kurdistan more than 2,500 years ago. At that time, different groups of people were moving around in search of good land. The people who stayed in that area slowly formed a common language. They became close-knit and fiercely loyal to each other because they were in a mountainous area that made it hard for other people to reach them.

Today, some Kurds still herd cattle, goats, horses and sheep, and they move around with their animals. Many of these Kurds live in tents made of black felt. They make the felt by crushing sheep wool with their feet. Most Kurds, though, are farmers and do not travel.

The Kurds have never had their own country or government. They have had different tribal or clan chiefs as leaders. Even today, families tend to pass on leadership.

There are probably 18 million to 20 million Kurds. That's at least twice as many people as are in Michigan. About half of the Kurds are in Turkey. In Iraq, there may be about 3 million to 4 million Kurds.

What happened to Gorbachev after the Soviet Union broke up?

Tamika Willis, Flint

Mikhail Gorbachev, who resigned as president of the Soviet Union before it broke up, opened a new office in Moscow.

He became the leader of the Gorbachev Institute, a private research group also called the Fund for Social and Political Research, a job allowing Gorbachev to study how countries and leaders make decisions.

He said he wasn't ready to retire from working at age 60. He did get some help from the new Russian government. He got a cottage, called a dacha (DACH-ah), in the country; 4,000 rubles (ROO-buls), which is about 40 American dollars, a month; two limousines, and up to 20 people assigned to be his security guards.

What kind of doctor is Jack Kevorkian?

Benjamin Jones, Detroit

Dr. Jack Kevorkian, who has been in the news because he has helped assist people in suicides, is a retired pathologist.

A pathologist is a doctor who studies diseases and how people's bodies are changed by them. Usually, a pathologist doesn't see any patients in an office visit. The main duties can involve looking at samples, such as blood and body fluids, using a laboratory.

Kevorkian used to work in hospitals. He examined the bodies of dead people to see how their illnesses affected them.

34

Several years ago, he decided to quit his job as a pathologist and study death and dying.

Although he is a doctor, he can't practice medicine anymore because Michigan medical officials took away his license.

What happened in Waco, Texas, in 1993?

Cerrome Oatman, Detroit

David Koresh said he was a religious leader. He lived with more than 80 other people in a group of apartments, called a compound, in Waco, Texas. People ate, slept and spent all of their time there without going other places.

On April 19, 1993, a fire destroyed the compound.

Here are the events that led up to the fire:

■ A shoot-out: Federal agents whose job was to check on weapons sales wanted to check out reports that the group was buying and storing lots of guns and other weapons. Koresh did not want them in the compound. Four agents were killed in a shoot-out on Feb. 28, and 11 were hurt. Some members of the Koresh group were believed hurt. To avoid more people getting hurt, federal agents waited so more people could leave the compound. By March 1, 10 children were released. Eleven more children and 14 adults were freed later.

■ The day of the fire: Agents didn't want to wait any longer. They got permission from Attorney General Janet Reno to use tanks on April 19 to break through the walls and pump in tear gas, which makes people cough and cry. Several people escaped before the fire started.

By Detroit Free Press staff

35

How many cults are there in the United States?

Kathy Murphy's Third-Grade Salk Elementary Class, Fraser

There could be anywhere from 600 to more than 1,000 cults. Part of the problem in giving a number is how to define what a cult is. In the past, the word has been used to cover any new religion or a group that broke the rules of the main religion. Here is how a cult, such as the group near Waco, Texas, is usually described: A group that is isolated — living apart from others — and that requires members to give up private property. Members also view most outsiders as evil or bad and support the leader's cause, no matter what the effect.

Did David Koresh grow up thinking he was Jesus?

Lorri Thomas, Detroit

No. Koresh prayed and read the Bible a lot. It wasn't until the last five years of his life that he began to call himself Jesus Christ. It was not clear whether he really believed he was Jesus, or whether he took that name to symbolize his leadership of the Branch Davidians, the religious group he was in charge of.

What state makes the most money from tourism?

Christen Kinsler, Sterling Heights

California makes the most money in tourism. Florida comes second and New York third. Michigan is No. 12 when counting money made from tourism.

California draws a lot of people because it has a

combination of things that interest tourists: natural places, such as beaches and mountains, mild weather, and places people have built, such as Disneyland.

Florida also draws people because of its good weather and beaches. But in Florida, the top three attractions are all from Disney: Epcot Center, Disney World and Disney MGM Studios. In New York, New York City has the most visitors; Niagara Falls is next. The third is the Corning Glass Center in the city of Corning, where glass is made and which has a museum.

In Michigan, three places that get the most visitors are the town of Frankenmuth, which is north of Flint; Henry Ford Museum and Greenfield Village in Dearborn, and the Sleeping Bear sand dunes on Lake Michigan, near Traverse City.

Can the shuttle be seen from Earth when it's dark?

Shannon Broughton Iles, Waterford Township

Yes, for some space shuttle flights, if you're in the right place at the right time.

Figuring when a shuttle will pass by involves a lot of facts: the time it took off; its speed, about 17,400 miles an hour; the time it takes to go around the Earth, usually about 90 minutes; and the Earth's turning.

To see the shuttle pass by, though, you need to be in darkness and the spaceship needs to be in sunlight, so the spaceship reflects light back toward you on Earth. That happens only at dawn or dusk.

Where is Saddam Hussein?

Torjorn Yervik, Norway, at camp in Wixom

Saddam (Sah DAM) Hussein (WHO sain) is in Baghdad, the capital of Iraq. He is believed to be living in the presidential palace. It is the home for the president of Iraq, just as the White House in Washington, D.C., is where the president of the United States lives.

The palace is believed to have three giant underground bunkers, which are rooms 60 feet underground. Hussein may have hidden there during the Persian Gulf War that began in January 1991.

How did American pilots in the Persian Gulf War know where the targets were?

Steven Goguen, Roseville

They'd seen pictures of them. Ever since 1960, the United States has had satellites that take pictures of the world as they orbit it. Have you ever seen the pictures that the weather people on television use? Those show where the clouds are and where it's raining. It's the same idea, except that the military is looking not for weather, but for buildings, tanks, planes or troops.

The satellites taking pictures of Iraq were put in space by

the space shuttle. They circle 100 to 300 miles above the Earth, but they can take pictures that show things very close up.

Another way the military found out where things were was by taking pictures of what they saw from airplanes. Lots of people working in the Middle East and in Washington, D.C., looked at photos and figured out what they meant. They compared them to pictures taken the day before to see whether anything had changed. They told the bomber pilots what to look for and where.

Sometimes the military used special cameras that could take pictures of heat. Then, even when a tank had been painted to look like the desert, it could be seen by the special cameras if its engine had been turned on or if its guns had been fired, because they gave off heat.

The U.S. military also had satellites and aircraft that could find radio waves. They looked for the radio waves that Iraqi generals used to talk to each other. When soldiers found those waves, they could find where they were coming from, then tell the air forces of the nations united against Iraq where to aim their bombs.

It was also possible that there were spies who told the military where bombs were being made, where chemicals were being created or where tanks were being built. But such information would be hard to get and hard to get out of an enemy country.

By Amy Wilson

Why are there so many earthquakes in California?

Monica Pilarski, Sterling Heights

California has a lot of earthquakes because of its location. The state is on the boundary of several plates, which is the word used to describe the upper parts of the Earth that move.

These are the areas where earthquakes are strongest and happen the most often.

Here's why:

A plate is an area that moves in only one direction. The edges of the plate are where the most earthquakes occur.

Along the edges, the Earth also gets many faults, or cracks.

Southern California is on the boundary, or edge, of two plates called the Pacific Plate and North American Plate. That's the San Andreas Fault.

The northern part of California, where quakes happened in April 1992, has a third plate, the Gorda Plate, with a different motion.

These plates moved in different directions against each other at a place people call the Mendocino Triple Junction, where several faults meet.

The stress of two or more plates moving against each other is always happening.

When pressure builds up, there is a bigger movement. That's when the faults or cracks break — which means the rocks in the earth break — and an earthquake occurs.

Scientists can't tell when this will happen.

Who carved Mt. Rushmore?

Renee Suzanne Rapley, Taylor

Artist Gutzon (GOOT-zen) Borglum (BORG-lum) designed the Mt. Rushmore National Memorial in the Black Hills of South Dakota that shows the faces of George Washington, Thomas Jefferson, Theodore Roosevelt and Abraham Lincoln.

It took 360 workers to do the carving on the granite cliff. They worked on and off for 14 years, beginning in 1927.

The work was stopped several times when there was no money to pay the workers.

Most of the workers were not artists. They were construction workers, drillers and miners. The mountain mostly was carved by dynamite.

A small model of the mountain was used to mark where the faces would go.

Sometimes the project supervisor was a sculptor or someone trained in art; but this wasn't detailed work — just carving George Washington's eye meant dynamiting out an 11-foot-wide hole. The nose is about 20 feet long.

Borglum died in 1941 before Mt. Rushmore was finished. His son, Lincoln, finished supervising the project.

Does Somalia have pollution?

Amy Coon, Lapeer

Yes, it has pollution. Fighting in that eastern African country has meant that people have not been able to move around safely as much as they used to. People who herded sheep and cattle to different lands for feeding have stayed in one area, overusing the land without giving it rest. This means the soil has not had a chance to restore its nutrients.

People have cut down trees for firewood as they have camped in these areas, leaving the soil open to damage from winds and the sun. The result of these changes in people's living patterns has been that the land is too dry and not usable for growing crops.

People who can't get enough food and water have gathered in groups near cities and feeding centers. The water has become unclean because of the large numbers of people and animals in one place. Trash and sewage have gotten into the water used for cooking, drinking and bathing and made people sick.

What is it like to live in Somalia?

Jessica Jenkins, Detroit

Most people spend their time trying to get food. Many adults also spend time taking care of sick children or other sick adults.

For families who have little or no food, each day involves waking up and sometimes packing up their belongings and traveling toward towns where food may be delivered. At a feeding center, they will get rice or beans. For those who have some animals, meals could include camel's milk or goat's meat.

Many people suffer from diseases that come from unclean water and food. There are not many places to wash, though some villages and cities have wells.

Before U.S. and other troops arrived, walking in cities and villages meant Somalians had to watch out for gunfire and for people who might steal their food.

At night, people may sleep in a tent-like hut covered with grass mats and animal skins. Others sleep in any shelter they can find.

Why do people shoot themselves after killing someone?

Melvin Hawkins, Detroit

No one knows exactly why. Each situation is different when there is a death, but there are some reasons it happens more when one person in a family kills someone else in the family.

In families or among people who live together closely, there are strong feelings. There is strong love, but there can also be very angry and hateful feelings.

A shooting or killing in this case usually is sudden and happens when one person loses control of his or her angry feelings.

That person is confused about those feelings and wants to hurt someone. If the person who loses control has a gun at home, it makes it easier to put those feelings into action.

After any shooting has occurred, that person can be:

■ Afraid of punishment or wanting to punish himself or herself before somebody else does.

■ Feeling helpless.

■ Sorry and worried over the action, but confused about what to do next.

All those feelings happening at once can make a person not want to live after shooting someone in the family.

When the census is taken every 10 years, how do they count the homeless?

Hilary Alpert, Troy

People who take the census — a count of the number of people in the United States — tried to count the homeless in 1990 in several ways:

■ They visited shelters, places where homeless people can find a bed and a meal.

■ They looked in places where homeless people live outdoors, such as under bridges.

■ They tried to find empty houses or other buildings where homeless people go to escape bad weather and to rest.

There is a lot of disagreement about the census numbers. In Detroit, some people believe close to 37,000 people — that's almost as many as live in the whole city of Jackson — probably weren't counted. Some of those were homeless people; others were people who had a place to stay but didn't want to give any information about themselves.

Census takers say they are looking at ways to improve counting people for the next census in 2000.

If you have an idea, you can write:

Director
Bureau of Census
Washington, D.C. 20233

Which children's television show is more popular — "Barney and Friends" or "Sesame Street"? How?

Matthew Zalewski, Madison Heights

In early 1993, "Barney and Friends" was the more popular of the two Public Broadcasting Service shows — if you define popularity by television ratings.

Here's how the popularity was measured: For one week in January 1993, the A.C. Nielsen company checked on "Barney" and "Sesame Street."

The Nielsen people measure the people who watch different shows by attaching a special meter to volunteers' television sets. (In the Detroit area, people just keep diaries, written records of what they watch.)

The device shows what station and show are being watched and who is watching. This sample is considered a way to estimate what all viewers watch.

In that week, for example, nearly four million homes watched the "Barney and Friends" show. About 2.5 million homes had on "Sesame Street" during the same week.

People at PBS, which is WTVS-TV (Channel 56) in Detroit, said both shows are popular and it's hard to draw big conclusions from one week.

The president

Why are presidents elected for only four years?

Melissa Webb, Canton Township

The founders of this country were afraid a president who would not be up for election regularly would become too powerful, and more like a king or queen than a leader responsible to the people.

They tried to choose a time that would be long enough for a leader to get experience and keep things in order.

Four years was the agreement between two sides that argued angrily at the meeting in the summer of 1787 when the founders set up rules for the U.S. Constitution.

Some people were really afraid of a powerful leader. They wanted a president who was up for election every year. Others were worried that everything would get very disorganized if the president didn't have enough time to make decisions or carry them through.

Why do we need a president?

Jackie Palinski, Sterling Heights

The United States needs a president because the people who started this country wanted someone to be in charge but didn't want a king or queen.

They had already had a king when they were ruled by England before 1776, and they didn't like that.

So they set up rules for a president in the U.S. Constitution (con-stih-TOO-shun).

When they set up the government, they divided it into three main parts, called branches:

■ The executive branch is the president, who is elected by the people every four years. The president is also commander in chief of the U.S. military.

■ The legislative branch is the Congress, which is the people elected to make laws.

■ The judicial branch is made up of the courts, which decide specific cases.

This three-part system allows for a leader who is chosen by the people and cannot become too powerful.

Electing a president every four years means the leader must listen to the people and be responsible for decisions that affect voters.

Why are the Republicans shown as elephants and Democrats as donkeys?

Bill Price, Lincoln Park

The donkey was believed to be first used as a mean name for a Democrat. In 1828, when Andrew Jackson was running for president, he was called a jackass, another word for someone who acts stupidly, and also a word for a donkey. Donkeys are considered stubborn animals. Jackson decided to use the donkey as his symbol because he was proud of being stubborn about some things.

But it became better known when a cartoonist, Thomas Nast (rhymes with last), used the donkey to represent newspapers that supported Democrats and that Nast thought were being stubborn and foolish. Nast liked to use animals in his cartoons to show either people or ideas.

By the late 1800s, the Democratic Party made the donkey its mascot, a symbol of the party.

The party doesn't use the symbol in its designs.

The elephant symbol for the Republican Party also goes back to Nast, who made it popular in 1874 in a cartoon. The cartoon shows an elephant, as a sign of Republican voters, frightened by a donkey dressed in a lion's skin. Soon after, an elephant became a symbol for the Republican Party. In 1969, the party made a modern elephant design its official symbol.

Why is the presidential election in November?

Brandi McClintock, Detroit

November was chosen as the time for a national election because it was after most of the farmers in the country had harvested the crops and before heavy snows might start in December. That gave the electors — the people named by political parties to elect a president — time to travel to their state capitals and vote.

The Constitution allows Congress to pick the date. In 1792, Congress made the first Wednesday in December the date for presidential electors to meet. That law also required the states to name their electors sometime within the 34 days beforehand.

Then, in 1845, Congress made it law that electors would be selected on the same day in November, "the first Tuesday after the first Monday."

Early in the week was considered a good time not to hurt business. People didn't want Sunday because they felt that would be doing business on a day of prayer.

How long does it take to count the votes for the presidential election?

Vanessa Miller, Lake Orion

It takes about 19 hours to get Michigan's unofficial vote count.

Most states are about the same.

The official count could take two or three weeks. By then the state is finished certifying — which means OKing — the vote totals after correcting any mistakes made as the votes were reported from precincts.

You often see results sooner in your newspaper and on television because of a system called sampling, whereby predictions are made based on only a part of the vote that is in.

Also, state totals are gathered together so you see who's the unofficial winner in the country. Usually this is correct, but in a close race, it's not always possible to get accurate predictions.

What is the electoral college? What do they do there?

Rebecca Hall, East Lansing

The electoral college is not a school like Michigan State University. "College," in this case, refers to a group of people who meet for one purpose. The name is not in the U.S. Constitution — it was the way journalists and other people started to describe the founders' plan in 1787 to pick a president.

The electors are a group of people who represent each state's votes.

The founders decided to use electors because they didn't think people were well informed about candidates. Instead, people would pick someone they knew from their state to make the decision. Communication was slow, and fewer people read than now, so it was harder to learn about the people running for president.

The founders wanted to protect each state's rights, so they wanted to soften the influence of states with a lot of people.

Nowadays, though, states such as California, for example, have a lot of electoral votes because the number of electors is based on a state's number of members in the Senate and the House of Representatives.

These electors meet after the election in each state's capital to vote for their candidates.

Usually the electors are people who are very loyal to a party, such as the Democrats or the Republicans.

The 538 ballots from the electors in every state are officially counted in early January in Congress.

It takes 270 electoral votes for a candidate to win.

Why do people vote in early November when the decision is made later by electors?

Robert Gibson, Redford

People are really making a decision in November when they vote for a president.

But they are choosing a team of electors as well as a president. The electors for the main parties, Democrats and Republicans, are people who are loyal to the party.

It takes 270 electoral votes for a candidate to become the president.

Whichever candidate wins the state popular vote in November, that candidate's electoral team votes.

In Michigan, the electors must vote for the candidate they promised to vote for. The reason there is more than a month between the popular and electoral votes is because when the founders set up this system, it took time for the electors to travel to the state capital, on horseback or in carriages pulled by horses.

The reason electors were chosen to make the final vote is because of the belief more than 200 years ago that not many people knew much about the candidates.

Can the president's wife vote?

Kate Mancani, Sterling Heights

Yes, the president's wife can vote for any candidate, and she can keep her vote a secret if she wants to. That's the right of every voter. She could even vote against her husband if she wanted to.

No president's wife voted before 1920. That was the first year women were allowed to vote. The 19th Amendment to the U.S. Constitution had changed the rule that allowed only men to vote.

If a presidential election goes to the House of Representatives, what happens if there is a tie?

Chris Miller, Lake Orion

They just keep voting until they get a winner.

The only way a presidential election will go to the House of Representatives is if no candidate wins at least 270 electoral votes.

Electoral votes are the votes by each state's electors, people chosen to vote for the president.

If the election goes to the House, each state has one vote. If no one gets at least 26 votes, the House votes again.

If a president still isn't chosen by Jan. 20, the vice president-elect, who is chosen by the Senate, would become president.

If the Senate can't choose a vice president by Jan. 20, then the Speaker of the House becomes president.

After the president has been elected in November, how long does he have to wait before he can move in?

Pillar Moffitt, Woodhaven

A new president has to wait until after noon on Jan. 20 of the next year to move into the White House.

That date is the start of the president's term. The rule on that is written in the 20th Amendment to the Constitution.

Until then, the newly elected president is called the president-elect.

Why does the president who was elected for the next four years have to wait until Jan. 20 to get inaugurated?

Rachel Grossman, Farmington Hills.

Jan. 20 is the date set in the 20th Amendment to the U.S. Constitution.

There are reasons the Constitution calls for several months between the election and the inauguration, or swearing in, of the new president.

The election isn't official until each state's electors, the group of people who promised to vote for a candidate, meet in each state's capital and vote. Then those votes are sent to Washington, D.C., and are counted in front of Congress during the first week in January.

The inauguration used to be March 4. That changed in 1933 when the 20th Amendment was approved. The old date had provided for time to travel. People agreed that several months were no longer needed. Also, they believed that was too long to wait for a new president to take office. The Jan. 20 date still gives time for transition, for the president-elect to make plans to move and to name some of the people on his staff, and for the current president to prepare to leave.

What are the three main words in the inaugural oath?

Erica Montgomery, Detroit.

"Preserve," "protect" and "defend" often are considered key words.

"Preserve" means to keep and maintain something as it is now. "Protect" means to keep it safe from any damage. "Defend" means to fight anything that might hurt or destroy it.

How many of the presidents came from Michigan?

Emily Zeig, Sterling Heights

One. Gerald Ford, the 38th president.

He wasn't born in Michigan, but his family moved to the state from Nebraska in 1915 when he was 2.

He went to school in Grand Rapids, graduated from the University of Michigan and was one of Michigan's representatives in the U.S. House until he was named vice president in 1973. He became president in 1974 after President Richard M. Nixon resigned.

Ford ran for re-election in 1976 but was defeated by Jimmy Carter.

Was there a bald president?

Ivan Tarducci, Melvindale

No president appears to have been totally without hair. There do appear to have been lots of presidents with thinning hair. The average age for men taking presidential office in America is 55. That's late middle age, a time when most men's hair has started to thin. It's also a time when, if they are going to be bald when they are old, their hairlines have begun to recede, or draw back, so that you see more and more forehead and less and less hair.

Probably the presidents with the least hair were John Quincy Adams, Martin Van Buren, James Garfield and Dwight D. Eisenhower.

Of all the U.S. presidents, 11 have had really good heads of hair. Those would include John F. Kennedy, Jimmy Carter and Ronald Reagan.

by Amy Wilson

Who pays to air presidential addresses on TV?

Steven Grow, Maple City

Nobody.

It's free.

No network had to run the message from President George Bush in 1992 asking people to help victims of Hurricane Andrew, for example, but usually networks agree when the president's staff asks.

They did not consider it a political campaign message, which would be an advertisment.

When the networks plan for the message, they just move their programs back.

How much money does the president make in a year?

Ryan Miner, St. Clair

President Bush was paid $200,000 a year. He got a paycheck once a month.

Do presidents get retirement after their term?

Randi Jo Marshall, Vestaburg

Yes, they get pensions, a certain amount of money each year as a reward for having served in the job.

Former presidents also get services such as Secret Service protection, medical care and magazine subscriptions as long as they live. Presidents didn't always have pensions. The system started when President Harry Truman was going to leave office and didn't have any money of his own to live on. Congress approved a law that would give Truman and any other former president some money to live on and other privileges so he wouldn't have to find a new job.

Other former presidents, including George Bush, have their own money, but that doesn't change the law.

What do presidents do after their term has ended?

Daniel Storchan, West Bloomfield Township

They do whatever they want. Here are some recent examples:

Gerald Ford, who is from Michigan, plays golf as a hobby but also gives speeches to schools and other groups that would like to hear him talk about his years as president.

Ronald Reagan likes to relax by riding horses. He also gives speeches.

Jimmy Carter has been active in a group called Habitat for Humanity, which builds homes for poor people. He also has traveled to help foreign countries, including a trip to help make sure everybody got a chance to vote in an election in Zambia, a country in southern Africa.

Richard Nixon has written a book.

Why do they call the president's wife the "first lady"? Also the governor's wife?

Megan Renee Beyer, Sterling Heights

The words have not always been used to describe the president's wife.

"First lady" was believed to be first used in 1849, by President Zachary Taylor, to describe Dolley Madison, a former president's wife.

He called her the "first lady of the land" because she was so well-known as a hostess for important parties in Washington.

She was married to President James Madison, who served from 1809 to 1817.

The name as a title for the president's wife was used somewhat after the Civil War. That was a time when women had been in charge of homes, farms and businesses while many men had been fighting the war.

After the war, people began to pay more attention to women's roles, including the role of the president's wife.

In the 1900s, people began to look more at a president's wife as being an important partner in making decisions.

By then, "first lady" was used often. Now it is used for a president's wife and also often for the wife of a state governor.

Why is the White House in Washington?

Kimberly Johnson, Detroit

In 1790 that's where Congress decided to build a new city to contain all government buildings. Before then, President George Washington had lived in both New York City and Philadelphia.

There was a lot of disagreement, so President Washington helped choose the location. The new city was in a Southern area, but many considered it to be a place that would serve people in both the North and the South. It was set up as the District of Columbia, not a state, because Northern states did not want a capital in slave-holding Southern states. George Washington's own home, Mt. Vernon, was nearby, so he liked the location.

Do the relatives of the president live in the White House with him?

Kristina Trejo, Melvindale

That's up to the president.

Benjamin Harrison may be the president who had the most relatives living in the White House. He and his wife shared the White House with a married son and daughter, their spouses, three grandchildren, Mrs. Harrison's father and a niece.

What is it like to live in the White House?

Katie Cockrel, Detroit

For a president's family, it mainly means lots of attention and not a lot of privacy. Parts of the house are open for tours, and, of course, what a president's family does is reported in newspapers and on TV.

Some presidential sons and daughters have complained that all this attention meant living in the White House wasn't fun.

How many kids have lived in the White House?

Shakeita Avant, Detroit

At least 14 children (younger than 16) of presidents lived in the White House before Bill Clinton's daughter, Chelsea.

There have been more kids than that in the White House, though, because presidents' nieces, nephews and grandchildren also have lived there.

The first child born in the White House was James Madison Randolph, Thomas Jefferson's grandson, on Jan. 17, 1806.

What do kids do in the White House for fun?

Philip Bolus, Sterling Heights

President Theodore Roosevelt's family, which included six children, is still famous for roller-skating in the East Room, bicycle riding in the halls, having pillow fights and even taking a pony upstairs. President Woodrow Wilson's daughters were known for playing practical jokes.

More recently, Amy Carter had a tree house built on the White House lawn. She also roller-skated on sidewalks near the White House.

What was the most unusual pet in the White House?

Mija McMann, Detroit

Probably a badger, owned by President Theodore Roosevelt.

Roosevelt loved animals and had the biggest variety of them in the White House. He also had some of the wildest, including a bear cub. Theodore Roosevelt was president from 1901 to 1909.

President Herbert Hoover had many small creatures, including lizards, horned toads and frogs, in the White House.

He was president from 1929 to 1933.

How many bathrooms are in the White House?

Alexander Jacobs, Detroit

There are 32 bathrooms in the White House, where the president's family lives.

How many maids are in the White House?

Sarah Kovach, Wyandotte

Six maids take care of the house where the presidents and their families live.

They do the dusting, help with the laundry and change the sheets and blankets in the bedrooms.

When there have been children living in the White House, the maids have cleaned their rooms.

Nine housemen do heavy cleaning chores such as vacuuming and cleaning windows.

The president has a valet (val-LAY) who helps take care of his clothes and personal grooming.

Where does the vice president live? Does the government supply a house?

Lori Frazier, Lincoln Park

The vice president lives in a house on land that is part of the Naval Observatory in Washington, D.C.

Yes, the government supplies the house, which is owned by the Navy.

The house has been approved for use for the vice president since 1974. Before then, a vice president had a private home in Washington. The government would help pay expenses for security and some entertainment.

Originally, the house where vice presidents now live was built for the chief of the Naval Observatory. After that the chief of naval operations lived there.

In 1966, Congress approved a bill to build a new house for the vice president. But Congress didn't want to OK money to pay for building the new house, so in 1974 Congress suggested using the house of the chief of naval operations.

Gerald Ford would have been the first vice president to live there, but he moved into the White House as president when Richard Nixon resigned.

The first family to live there was the family of Walter Mondale, vice president for Jimmy Carter.

Did President George Bush own his own car?

Scott Follen, Mt. Clemens

When George Bush was president, he owned a 1986 Ford pickup and a 1986 Ford Bronco. He didn't drive them often and he didn't say where he kept them.

Most of the time, Bush rode in a limousine designed with special features, such as bullet-proof glass, to help protect him. The limousines were either Lincolns or Cadillacs. Bush sat in the back seat and a chauffeur drove.

How many vehicles does President Clinton have?

Josephine Liparoto, Rockwood

One. President Bill Clinton has a '68 blue Mustang convertible, but he doesn't usually drive it. He usually rides in a limousine.

WHERE TO WRITE

If you want to give advice to the president or vice president, you can write them yourself at these addresses. There is a special staff that helps answer mail from young people.

The President
The White House
1600 Pennsylvania Avenue
Washington, D.C. 20500

The Vice President
Old Executive Office Building
Correspondence Office
Washington, D.C. 20501

The environment

The world is made up of how much water?

JoiTonya Dunham, Detroit

Almost three-fourths of the Earth's surface is water. It's always had the same amount of water, but the water has moved around.

Of all that water, only 1 percent is fresh water, which is water that does not contain salt.

How do animals pollute the water?

Tmeka Hale, Detroit

Most pollution by animals is from their own body waste. That's true of birds, for example, such as Canada geese.

But usually that pollution, or dirt, is easy for water to break down. It's a problem when there's too much goose manure in one area, which changes the life and plants in the water.

That usually means humans are responsible. For example, people may plant grain that would draw more geese than usual to a particular place. Anything that draws more people or animals than usual to one place can change the makeup of the land or water.

Other creatures in the water also pollute. In the Great Lakes, the zebra mussel is a relatively new arrival.

The mussel doesn't need some of the material that it takes in from the water. So it expels wads of waste from the body, just as any living thing gets rid of what it doesn't need. A lot of these wads sometimes float to the bottom of the lake and remain in the water.

Mussels also may store bad chemicals in their tissue, and those bad chemicals keep moving up toward humans through the food chain if the mussels are eaten by other fish. Or the mussels and their bad chemicals may end up dead on the sand, polluting the beaches and the water.

There are other ways in which water becomes dirty:

■ In oceans, squid shoot off ink as a way to defend

themselves.

■ On land, beavers sometimes put trash in the water when making a beaver dam, which changes the water flow, too.

It's generally considered pollution when any of these natural materials is present in such a big quantity that it hurts the quality of the water.

I want to know whether you can eat zebra mussels.

Emily McClintock, Mt. Clemens

No, you shouldn't eat this type of mussel.

Most of the zebra mussels in the Great Lakes have germs found in wastewater and poisons such as pesticides inside them. That's because many of these mussels live near pipes where waste from factories and cities is put into the water.

Even if you found some zebra mussels in clean water, you probably wouldn't want to eat them. These mussels are small, less than one-inch wide, and would be hard to get out of the shell. They taste awful, say people who have tried them.

The mussels you can eat are found in oceans. The two main kinds sold in stores and to restaurants are the Atlantic blue mussel and the green-lipped mussel.

Any mussels that have come from water where they might pick up germs would not be allowed to be sold.

What is the U.S. government doing to reduce the greenhouse effect?

Vijay Saluja, Sault Ste. Marie

The U.S. government has been doing nothing — directly — about the greenhouse effect, the trapping of gases that would cause the Earth's climate to become warmer.

Everybody, including some U.S. leaders and some people who study climate, has not been in agreement about how big a problem this is. Although there is no law that accepts this as a problem and sets rules on the greenhouse effect, there are government rules that set limits on some of the six gases believed to contribute to warming the atmosphere.

The Clean Air Act is the main law that limits air pollution, including gases from cars, air-conditioners and factories.

The people who set the goals for environmental laws say it would be very costly to cut all global warming gases, and they aren't ready to make a law. They want to encourage the study of other fuels and urge more people to cut back on pollution.

Why isn't the Rouge River clean? When will the Rouge River be cleaned?

Joe Kramer and Heidi Wegmueller, Dearborn

One big problem is waste water from city sewers.
Waste water from nearly 50 towns sometimes goes into

the Rouge. If heavy rain fills up the sewer, it means that sewage (anything put down the drain or toilet) can end up in the river along with storm water. The sewage water contains bacteria that make it harmful to your health.

The Michigan Department of Natural Resources has a plan that requires cities to change the way the sewer system works. Its goal is to complete the plan in 2005. Some ideas are to have a storage place for extra water and different systems for sewage and storm water. The cities need to decide who will clean the water and how to pay for changes in the sewer system. Another thing keeping the Rouge River from being clean is runoff — water that flows from the ground into the Rouge, draining chemicals and manure from farms and extra dirt from construction projects.

A group called Friends of the Rouge River works with high school students to test the water.

Are there holes in the ozone layer?

Eric Cortright, Sterling Heights

There are no actual holes in the ozone layer, just places where the amount of ozone in the atmosphere is very small at certain times of the year. In recent years, one such thin spot has been appearing over the South Pole, the southernmost point of the Earth. It shows up for a few months, then goes away. Scientists were worried that a similar thin spot would appear over the North Pole, the northernmost point of the Earth, last year, but it didn't.

By Emilia Askari

Why don't they put garbage in the shuttle and let it take it up to the sun and burn up there?

Jeri Miccolis, Sterling Heights

There are two big reasons people can't shoot trash into the sun — or to Mars or even the moon.

First, there's too much of it. A space shuttle can carry 65,000 pounds of cargo into orbit. That sounds like a lot, but it's not much when you compare it to the 875 million pounds of trash Americans throw away every day. That 875 million pounds would fill a 30-story building as wide as three football fields.

There are not many American space shuttles. Each time one of them goes into orbit, which is the path the shuttle takes around the Earth, and then lands, it takes several months to get it ready to take off again. But 10,000 shuttles blasting off every day wouldn't be enough to get rid of all our trash.

The second reason we can't do it is that it would cost way too much.

By Mike Williams

Why do birds die when oil gets on them?

Heather Brown, Detroit

There are several reasons why birds die when oil gets on their feathers:

When a bird is covered with oil, the feathers get matted down and can't trap air to keep the bird warm. Like the down coats many people wear in winter, downy feathers help keep birds warm by trapping air around their bodies and keeping their skin dry. When the feathers get all stuck together, water is able to seep through to the bird's skin, making the bird even colder.

Fluffy feathers also help birds float, swim and fly. With oily feathers, they may drown or starve because they can't move around to get food. Or they may get killed by other animals because they can't get away fast enough.

When a bird gets dirty, it tries to clean its feathers with its beak. In the process, a bird that is covered with oil may eat the oil, get sick and die.

By Nancy Ross-Flanigan

How did the oil well fires in Kuwait in 1991 add to the problem of acid rain?

Vijay Saluja, Sault Ste. Marie

The oil well fires in Kuwait added soot, gases and acids to the air. Acids are chemical compounds. A mild acid is lemon juice. Acid rain is created when chemicals such as sulfur dioxide from the oil fires are released into the air, then rain down as sulfuric acid.

After the Persian Gulf War in 1991, when were the people of Kuwait and Iraq able to go out of their houses in spite of all the pollution?

Roxanne Hallums, Mt. Clemens

Most of the people in Kuwait and Iraq went outside all the time, even in polluted air; but in Kuwait, people with asthma and other breathing problems may have had to stay inside on days when the wind was blowing soot from oil well fires in their direction. Usually, the winds shifted the worst of the fires' smoke to the southern part of Kuwait. That air was very different from the air in places such as Los Angeles and Detroit, which have pollution. It was so different that people who checked pollution levels found they needed to change some of their equipment to measure the bigger particles from the fires.

The air was sometimes so black from oil soot that at noon it was like midnight, and drivers had to turn on their headlights. The Kuwait government wanted people to use masks outside because no one knew the long-term health risks.

Nature

Why is spring called spring?

Dana Sellers, Detroit

"Spring" as a word for the season began to be used about 400 years ago in England because it meant to leap up, or rise.

In the English language, it first was used for water rising — or springing from the ground. The idea of rising soon was used for other things, such as the beginning of the day.

By the 1500s, people used the word "spring" to mean the first season or beginning of a new year of growth.

Why is the robin the first bird of spring?

Annette Griffin, Detroit

The American robin is one of the first birds of spring because it comes back from the southern part of America — places such as North Carolina, Tennessee and Texas — when there are signs that spring is beginning.

For birds, those signs are more hours of daylight, warmer weather and more bugs on the ground.

Because robins eat ground bugs, they come back earlier than birds that eat only flying bugs, which come out when the weather is even warmer.

But robins are not a very reliable way to be sure spring weather has arrived. Some robins stay in Michigan all winter, eating berries and eating from bird feeders people have in their yards. Some robins turn around and go back south if the weather turns cold again.

Why are plants green?

Leah Ezzell, Birmingham

The color of green plants comes from something called chlorophyll (KLOR-uh-fill). The chlorophyll is inside special parts of leaves where the plant's food is made. It helps the plant trap light and convert it into a form of energy the plant can use to nourish itself.

If you've ever looked at a tiny, young plant, you may have noticed that the leaves are very pale and often are not even green at first. They turn a rich green only as the plant gets older. That's because the plant doesn't make its own food at first — it lives on food stored in the seed from which it grew. The chlorophyll doesn't form until the plant is ready to start making its own food.

Some plants, such as evergreen trees, stay green year-round. Others, such as maple trees, change color with the season and drop all their leaves. That's because the plants stop making chlorophyll in the fall, as they prepare to go into a resting stage. As long as chlorophyll is being made, it covers up other natural colors in the leaves. But when the plants stop making chlorophyll, the other colors show up.

By Nancy Ross-Flanigan

Why do they call plant people "green thumbs"?

Jilliann Hughes, Southgate

People who work with plants have been said to have green thumbs — or green fingers — for more than 100 years because they get their hands into the dirt, green grass or green leaves of plants.

The words "green thumb" may have been patterned after "goldenthumb," which was once used to describe millers in England. Millers ground grain, which was golden, and their jobs sometimes made them wealthy, bringing them gold coins, just as skilled gardeners' getting their hands green results in green, healthy plants.

One British garden writer in the 1920s used the expression "green thumb" quite often, which made it popular.

For several years now, the word "green" by itself has been used to refer to people who are working to make the environment better or supporting changes that limit use of resources in the environment.

How tall will sunflowers grow?

Chris Fryer, Westland

Sunflowers can grow as tall as 12 feet. That's about three times as tall as an 8-year-old. The flowers can be as wide as 1 foot across.

Those are the giant sunflowers. Many sunflowers that grow in home gardens are from 8 to 10 feet tall.

Sunflowers grow well with rain and hot weather. By mid-August, most sunflowers have stopped growing. In September, a sunflower produces its seeds.

What is a forest?

Alan Walker, Detroit

A forest is any large area of land where the main plant is a tree. That includes cities.

The Detroit area is a large urban forest — where trees are the most common plant species. Trees don't have to be close together to make a land a forest.

Michigan used to be covered with enough forests that a squirrel could have crossed the state without coming down from the treetops.

Today about half of Michigan is called forested land. That includes land where the forest is managed to produce usable goods, such as wood and paper, as well as to protect wildlife.

Why does the moon change color? Why does a full moon sometimes look much bigger than usual?

Eric Moberg, Saline

The moon doesn't really change color; it just looks that way. The moon's surface is mainly gray.

When you see an orange or a red moon, for example, you are seeing that color through the Earth's air. You are seeing sunlight, which is reflected on the moon. Sunlight is many colors, but particles in the air take away the blue light, leaving the orange and red.

The time you see that color is when the moon sets or rises. That's when it is low in the sky and you see the color through the thicker parts of the air closer to Earth.

A hazy night with lots of pollution, for example, might make the moon more red or orange.

As for size, when a full moon is low in the horizon, it looks larger. Some people say it's because you're seeing it closer to ordinary objects, such as buildings and trees, so it looks bigger.

A good way to look at the moon's size is to look at it through an empty paper towel tube. First look at it on the horizon, when the moon is rising.

Then look again an hour later when it looks smaller to your eye. Looking through the cardboard tube, you will see it fills the same amount of space in your viewer.

Could we somehow generate electricity by the power of volcanic eruptions?

Laura Porteous, Reed City

Nobody is directly using an actual eruption's power — trying to control that could be very dangerous. However, people are using a kind of volcanic power for electricity. The heat in the Earth, in the form of steam, boiling water and hot rocks, is called geothermal energy. It can provide power for heat or electricity, among other uses.

Countries such as Iceland use geothermal power for steam heat piped into cities. People drill down, as they would for an oil well, to the ground's water. Usually the water is so hot that it's steam. That steam is fed through equipment that helps generate power.

Geothermal power plants usually are located where melted rock or steam is easy to reach with a drill. That would be in volcanic or earthquake areas. In the United States, geysers north of San Francisco provide some geothermal power.

In the Philippines, people had drilled for geothermal power at Mt. Pinatubo, the volcano that erupted in 1991, but had decided it wasn't practical to have a power plant there.

Why do volcanoes erupt?

Paul Kokeny, Mt. Clemens

The inside of the Earth is in constant motion and is heated. Deep in the Earth are patches of molten (MOLE-ten), which means "melted," rock. This hot liquid rock is usually held in place by the solid rock layers above it.

When the rock layers split or move, that can create openings for the molten rock. Because the molten rock is lighter than the rock around it, it tries to move up.

The molten rock also has gases inside it, which try to escape. Those gases help the molten rock move and fill any opening or split in the rock layers.

An explosion, such as the one in Japan on June 3, 1991, happens when the molten rock and its expanding gases build up.

The explosion is similar to what happens when you shake a can of soda pop, which also has gas in it. When the can is opened, the gas rapidly escapes, forcing the liquid out, too. The molten rock comes flying out the same way.

Weather

How does the weather change so quickly?

David Hinkle, Mt. Clemens

Fast-changing weather happens because of how the air moves. It happens a lot in the spring in Michigan. That's because there's a battle going on between cold air from the Arctic and warm air from the tropics. Michigan is often a battle zone because it's in the middle of a large, flat area with nothing to stop the cold and warm air from either direction.

What was the highest temperature in Michigan and do people get hurt by the temperature?

Nadia Helen Amen, Dearborn

The hottest day in Michigan was 112 degrees on July 13, 1936. It was recorded in the town of Mio, which is east of Grayling in northern Michigan.

People can be hurt in two main ways from how the body responds to heat. One way is heat exhaustion, which is caused by the blood trying to cool off the body. When outside temperatures get into the 90s, the brain sends the blood toward the skin, the outermost area, to cool it off.

When a person exercises too much, other parts of the body — the brain, the kidneys and the liver — don't get enough blood. That can cause people to feel dizzy, not think well, have stomachaches or faint. Babies and older people are usually affected the most often.

Another way heat can hurt is that the body can lose water. The brain tells the body to sweat, taking away the heat from the body by letting the water out through the skin. The body needs water to operate and if too much goes out through sweat, and the water and the salt in it aren't replaced, a person can become ill.

How do thunderstorms build up?

Adam Charles Teasdale, Wixom

Two main ingredients — heat and moisture — help form storms.

Usually, thunderstorms build up in front of cold air, such as a cold air mass coming down from Canada. That cold air pushes into the warm air. Sometimes, in places near water, that could be cold air moving off a lake.

As cold air moves in, the warm air is forced to rise. As air rises, it cools, usually 10 degrees Fahrenheit for every 1,000 feet, and expands.

In an ordinary rainstorm, the moisture-filled air is lifted and cooled until it can't hold the moisture it contains, so it has to release the moisture in the form of cloud droplets, which can grow into raindrops.

In a thunderstorm, the moist air is carried even higher. The warm, wet air rises and turns into a cloud, which grows quickly. The heat from the forming cloud makes the air rise even higher, into a long, narrow tower. The air gets so high that the water in it freezes. Because that cloud now has water and ice in it, electrical charges are set up, setting the stage for lightning.

How long is a baseball game held up due to rain?

Scott Fryer, Westland

There's no limit on how long a delay can be. It's up to the head umpire.

If a game is going to be called because of rain, then the delay must be at least 30 minutes first.

If the rain is before the game, it's up to the general manager of the home team to decide whether the weather or conditions of the field make it unsuitable for playing.

A rain delay is often anywhere from an hour to two hours, but delays have been longer.

Since 1950, the major baseball leagues have had a rain delay rule giving the umpire the right to decide. In earlier years, if a rain delay lasted longer than 30 minutes, that ended the game.

The main goal for umpires is always to complete the game, so they'll try to wait as long as possible.

Here is what helps an umpire decide whether to keep waiting out the rain or to end the game:

■ Weather forecast: The umpire keeps in touch with local forecasters who know how long a storm may last.

■ Type of field — artificial turf or grass: Turf is often quicker to drain.

■ The likelihood of injuries to players because of a wet field.

■ The baseball schedule: Late in the season, it's hard to fit in another game. A home team's schedule is also considered.

When the power goes out in a storm, how does Detroit Edison decide who gets power turned on first?

Kevin Ray and Jeffrey Ray, Detroit

The first customers to get electrical power back are places such as hospitals and police and fire departments because they take care of the health and safety of lots of people. Everyone says these places should have the highest priority (pry-OR-uh-tee). That means they get to go first. Priority is like rank. The higher your priority, the sooner you get service.

After that, the electric company works on making repairs that will help the most people all at once. For example, if your house is one of thousands in an area that lost power because of a storm, you'll probably have a higher priority than people in an area where only a few houses lost power.

That usually means people who live in big neighborhoods in the city will get their power back before people who live in the country.

But it doesn't automatically mean Detroit will get power before a smaller city. Edison provides electricity in six regions, including Macomb and Oakland counties. Each region sets up its own list of priorities.

Why was there a drought in California in 1991?

Matthew Zimmer, Birmingham

California's drought (DROWT) was the result of five years with a lot less rain and snow than usual.

California gets a lot of its water from the snow pack that builds each year in the Sierra Nevada Mountains in the eastern part of the state. The snow pack is a good kind of water because it melts slowly, giving a flow for a long period. That year, the snow pack was only about a third of what it normally is.

There was less rain and snow because of the jet stream, a band of fast-moving air currents high in the atmosphere. Storms follow the jet stream, and the jet stream had been sending storms away from California. Scientists say it's tough to predict what the jet stream will do.

A drought is defined as a dry spell that lasts long enough to damage crops. That is what happened in California. It affected people in Michigan because it cost more to buy fruit and vegetables since there were fewer of them available.

Michigan last had a drought in August 1988.

Why doesn't flooding Mississippi River water just flow downstream to the Gulf of Mexico? Why did the Mississippi River flood in 1993?

Casey Tonkin, East Jordan

The Mississippi is always flowing downstream. But when water fills the river faster than it flows down, the river can flood its banks.

It's natural for any river to flood regularly. The flat land on either side of a river or stream is called a flood plain. That is the place where floodwaters regularly rise, then later drop. People used to keep their houses and towns out of flood plains.

One of the reasons why the Mississippi River flooded so much during the summer of 1993 was that there was much more rain than usual in the states surrounding the Mississippi. Some places had rain each day for close to 5 weeks.

Water in the land and in all the other streams and rivers empties into the Mississippi. When those streams and rivers carry more water than usual, the Mississippi gets that water. The basin of land that drains into the Mississippi is two-thirds of the land of the United States, from roughly between the Rocky Mountains on the west and the Appalachian Mountains on the east.

(Michigan's rivers are part of the Great Lakes Basin, and they flow into the lakes surrounding the state.)

In 1993, parts of that land got more than a year's worth of rainfall in just two months.

The river kept flowing but couldn't take all the water fast enough, so the water needed to move outside the river's banks as well as flowing downstream.

Could the Detroit River overflow as the Mississippi River did in 1993?

Nicholas Stewart, Sterling Heights

No.

The Detroit River is more of a pipeline, or channel, connecting Lakes St. Clair and Erie.

It isn't a big drain for other rivers, as the Mississippi River is.

For example, smaller rivers in the states of Illinois, Iowa and Missouri flow into the Mississippi.

When rain made the waters rise in all the rivers, they poured into the Mississippi.

Although walls, or levees, protected some towns, they also added to the flooding at some spots, because the water had fewer places, such as wetlands, to spread out.

In Michigan, when extremely heavy rains raise the level of the lakes, the Detroit River rises, too.

Both Lake Erie and Lake St. Clair have flooded. Lake St. Clair is the smaller lake, so floods affect it first.

What causes hurricanes?

Joey King, Royal Oak

There are several ingredients that go into making a hurricane.

It usually starts with light showers in an area where air is moving in more than one direction.

For a hurricane to grow, this air needs to travel over ocean water that is at least 80 degrees warm from the surface to 200 feet below. As the air picks up heat and moisture from the ocean, thunderstorms often occur. The thunderstorms create even more heat. As the storms release heat, the weight, or pressure, of the air is lessened at the surface. Air at the surface spirals or spins, forming a column of air as high as 10 miles.

The column is the center of the storm. As the column gets hotter and wetter, the air on the ocean surface spins faster.

The spinning air feeds more heat and moisture to the center column. That's how a hurricane grows stronger.

Heat and moisture are what feed a hurricane or tropical storm. In the northern half of the world, where the United States is, the surface air for these storms spins counterclockwise, or opposite the direction the hands on a clock turn.

This gives the hurricane a whirlpool effect. The air spins much in the same way that water spins when you pull a plug in your bathtub drain.

A hurricane can keep growing until something breaks up the motion. This happens if the heat and moisture feeding the storm are cut. That can occur over colder water or when the storm meets with land.

Why are hurricanes always on the East Coast and never on the West Coast?

Andrea Rumsey, Livonia

The West Coast of the United States is too cold for hurricanes.

Hurricanes need seawater that is a temperature of at least 80 degrees Fahrenheit to grow. The part of the Pacific Ocean on the West Coast of the United States isn't that warm.

Even in colder parts of the Atlantic Ocean, a storm can follow the Gulf Stream, a current of warm water.

Warm water evaporates into warm air, which is a big part of what makes tropical storms grow. Storms get heat in the form of energy during that evaporation.

The more heat that enters the air, the more the air rises. The whirling winds of a storm pick up speed as they pick up warm air.

Storms can become hurricanes as winds increase and as storms pick up more warm, moist air. A storm becomes a hurricane once the winds near the center reach at least 74 miles per hour.

Only six out of 10 tropical storms each year in the Atlantic Ocean become hurricanes. Usually only two or three of the hurricanes hit the United States. That's because when they hit land or colder water, the winds start to drop off.

Was the hurricane in Hawaii in September 1992 as bad as the one in Florida that August?

Melissa Prado, Dearborn Heights

No, it wasn't.

Andrew, which hit south Florida and part of Louisiana, was worse than Iniki (ee-NEE-kee), which hit the island of Kauai (kah-WAH-ee).

Here are some of the ways Andrew was worse:

Stronger winds: Andrew had winds averaging 140 miles per hour. Iniki's winds averaged 130 miles per hour.

In terms of rankings by the National Weather Service, Andrew was a No. 4 level hurricane, with 5 being the worst category. Iniki was on the borderline between 3 and 4.

Andrew hit an area with more people — close to four million — while Kauai has only 52,000. Even if the storms had been the same strength, Andrew would be considered worse because it hit an area with more people.

How do hurricanes get their names?

Patty Foshia, Ferndale

Hurricanes are given names by the World Meteorological Organization, an international group of people who track and forecast the weather around the world.

The naming in the United States began in 1953 when the National Weather Service started using female names to make storms easier to remember than by the codes or numbers that had been used before. At first, the pilot in the plane tracking the storm was allowed to pick the name and often named it after his wife or girlfriend. Later, a weather service committee began picking the names. In 1979, men's names were added. Later, foreign names were included.

In the last several years, the World Meteorological Organization began handling the names. It makes sure the names reflect all of the world's cultures. Different storm areas, such as the north Atlantic Ocean or the eastern Pacific Ocean, get their own groups of names.

A storm is given a name from the assigned list when it is a tropical storm, which means a cluster of thunderstorms over warm ocean water with winds about 38 miles per hour. It becomes a hurricane when it has winds of 75 miles per hour and an "eye," which is a calm, cloud-free center.

A name that becomes famous from a storm, such as Hurricane Hugo, which hit the Carolinas in 1989, or Hurricane Andrew, which hit Florida in 1992, is retired and not used again.

If the names of hurricanes go in alphabetical order, why did Iniki come after Andrew?

Amanda Gifford, Adrian

Iniki (ee-NEE-kee), the hurricane that hit the Hawaiian island of Kauai (kah-WAH-ee) in September 1992, was taken from a list of names for hurricanes in the central Pacific Ocean; Andrew, which hit south Florida and part of Louisiana in August 1992, came from a list of names for the Atlantic Ocean.

Both lists are in alphabetical order. But the central Pacific list uses the Hawaiian alphabet, which has 12 letters (A, E, H, I, K, L, M, N, O, P, U, W). Weather people from around the world help name tropical storms; they pick names to match the languages and culture in an area. They put the names into four groups to match four areas of oceans.

The central Pacific group is for the region of ocean near the Hawaiian islands.

Andrew was the first hurricane in the Atlantic Ocean that year; Iniki was the fourth tropical storm or hurricane in the central Pacific that year.

Why do tornadoes always hit mobile home parks?

Pam Ritter, Center Line

Tornadoes don't always hit mobile home parks, but it may seem like they do. Actually, tornadoes hit other houses and buildings as often as they hit mobile homes.

But you probably hear most about tornadoes hitting mobile

homes because that's where half of all the deaths caused by tornadoes happen.

A mobile home offers very little protection against a tornado. There is no basement for people to stay in, and a mobile home is not very strong. So when a tornado hits an area where there's a mobile home park, it's likely to tear up the homes. Because mobile homes are parked close together, damage can happen when one home hits another or pieces of them shoot around.

Mobile home parks are often set up on flat, open land, where there are no tall buildings to block high winds.

How come so many people died in the cyclone in Bangladesh in April 1991 and not that many people die in a tornado here?

Tara Subbarao, Rochester Hills

A tornado in the United States is not the same kind of storm as the cyclone that hit Bangladesh.

The Bangladesh cyclone was what people here would call a hurricane, a violent tropical storm with heavy rain and a spiral of winds moving 74 miles per hour or faster.

Bangladesh, which is about the size of Wisconsin, is at sea level, and that means flooding and tidal waves easily sweep over land. There are not many safe places to escape.

Infections cause deaths, too. Diseases such as cholera spread quickly in Bangladesh because people don't have clean water to wash up. In a crowded country, infections can pass from person to person quickly.

People also die of starvation.

Why do leaves fall earlier some years?

Anna Kohn, Huntington Woods

Sometimes, trees' leaves fall earlier than usual because of dry weather in the summer.

A summer that is very hot and dry creates a lot of stress for trees. One way trees react to stress is to lose their leaves.

Also, for healthy trees, the temperature is a big factor that influences the leaves' color change and when they fall off.

Cooler than normal fall weather probably will speed up some of the color change. Also, an early warm spell in spring means leaves grow earlier, so the fall color change is likely to be ahead of schedule, too.

Another reason some leaves fall earlier is disease.

Why can you see your breath when you breathe in cold weather?

Scott Hobart, Harper Woods

What you are seeing are tiny water droplets in the air.

When you exhale, or breathe out, you are sending out water in the form of a gas. Your body, especially your lungs, needs moisture to work.

Of the gases you exhale, water is less than 1 percent. You can't see this gas until it hits the cold air.

But when the warm, wet air (98 degrees) of your breath meets with colder air, the water particles or molecules form into droplets of water. These droplets gather together, and that is what you see.

It doesn't last long, because the gas changes to liquid and then changes back to gas very quickly.

When the air is warmer, that moisture remains a gas that you don't see.

How is it that the National Weather Service is able to predict blizzard warnings so far in advance?

Heather Wilson, Highland

Blizzard or winter storm warnings are actually not given very far ahead, not much more than two days beforehand.

Here's how a forecast works:

Computers help make forecasts for storms.

A large computer just outside of Washington, D.C., is given information on weather patterns around the country. That information comes from satellites and weather-watch centers.

People check the computer forecasts and — from their own studies of the weather — figure out what's most likely to occur.

In Ann Arbor, National Weather Service people look at maps and then check to see how a weather pattern will affect Michigan.

Forecasters could be pretty sure about a storm with these signs, for example:

A low-pressure mass of air is headed this way. This type of air is like a funnel. It sucks up moisture as it moves along. An air mass is moving along this side of the mountain range called the Appalachians, in the eastern United States. Because it is a very large mass of air, forecasters know from previous patterns it is likely to head north. The temperatures in Michigan are going to be in the 20s and 30s, and that means the moisture will come down as snow.

101

Why are there no two snowflakes that look alike?

Tara Paulick, Royal Oak

Each snowflake has a different pattern because each ice crystal that groups together with others to make a flake is different. There is no limit to the combinations of crystal patterns, though scientists do classify snowflakes by general shape, such as column-like shapes, needle shapes or six-sided shapes.

A crystal's shape and growth are affected mainly by the temperature of the air around the crystal and the moisture in the air. Many crystals are so tiny you can't see them; even most snowflake patterns can't be seen well without a microscope.

❄ SNOWFLAKES

They start when water particles combine in cold air to form crystals. As the crystals form, they cling to particles of dust in the air. The cyrstals grow as more ice gets layered on, and then they become so heavy they fall to the earth. If the air is 32 degrees or colder, they remain frozen and come down as snowflakes.

After the crystals combine to make a snowflake, other factors influence how it is shaped. Among them: Wind can break flakes apart. Dry wind can take parts away by taking out the moisture. A wet wind can cause more ice to grow in the crystals. The way it spins can change the shape. For example, a flat, six-sided snowflake comes down from the sky sideways. The ends can break off and fall away. That forms new flakes and new patterns on the original flake.

Health

Why do bug bites itch or irritate your skin?

Emilie Oswald, Berkley

Bites from bugs that you encounter in summer — such as mosquitoes or black flies — itch because of the saliva the bugs leave in your blood.

When a black fly bites you, for example, it puts its saliva into your blood to keep the blood from thickening. That way, the bug can feed on your blood better.

In fact, usually when you interrupt the feeding by swatting away the fly, more saliva gets left in your blood — along with more of an itch. When a fly has finished feeding, there is less saliva, or spit-like substance, because the bug has sucked it up.

Because the saliva does not belong in your body, your body tries to fight it, and that's what actually makes it feel itchy.

What is Lyme disease?

Julie DiFranco, Mt. Clemens

Its name comes from the town of Old Lyme, Connecticut, where the illness was first described and recognized.

Lyme disease isn't something you catch from another person. People get it if they are bitten by a deer tick that is carrying the disease.

The deer tick, which lives on animals such as white-tailed deer and white-footed mice, drinks the blood of people and animals. When it bites a person, it can transfer germs or bacteria it has carried from an infected animal to the person.

The illness has different signs. People can have a fever, chills, a headache and a spreading rash that looks like a target with a bull's-eye.

Lyme disease also can cause serious problems such as paralyzing a person's arms or legs. It can be treated and cured by medicine, especially if it is spotted early.

In Michigan, the disease and the ticks that carry it are especially common in Menominee County, which is next to Wisconsin in the Upper Peninsula.

How could salmonella poisoning cause problems in cookie dough?

Chris Roebuck, Bloomfield Hills

This type of food poisoning can come from a raw egg used in some cookie dough. Salmonella is a tiny living organism that can live in the egg. You can't see or taste it. It's a type of bacteria and it can make people sick.

Not all eggs have salmonella, but to be safe, don't eat cookie dough. Wait until after the cookies are baked.

Cookies are safe then because the heat from baking kills bacteria.

By Jeanne Sarna

Is it healthy to eat snow?

Lesley Kulirak, Westland

No.

Although pure snow — which is crystals of water — would not be harmful, most snow around cities isn't clean.

You can't catch serious diseases from eating snow, but you can get sick from eating polluted snow.

Snow may have:

■ germs that harbor viruses. The germs can come from pollution in the air, from animals and litter. These germs can't be seen. Even a patch of fresh snow that appears to look clean may contain germs.

■ small objects — such as pine needles, gravel or other materials that would be harmful to swallow — buried in it.

Why did the government adopt 5 new food groups in 1992?

Rachael Garfinkle, West Bloomfield Township

The groups themselves — grains, dairy, meat, fruit and vegetables — were not new. The government has recommended choosing food every day from the five groups since 1980.

But many people still remember the government's information from the 1950s. That listed four food groups: Meat, fruit and vegetables as one group, dairy, and bread or grains.

In 1992, the government approved a new food guide on the five groups and a new way to show the groups in a pyramid shape.

The groups and the pyramid are supposed to help show the right foods to eat — and how much. A pyramid was chosen because it also shows what you need less of at the top and what you need to eat a lot of at the bottom.

The pyramid stresses three things:

- how much of each type of food you need daily;
- what different foods you need from each main food group;
- what type of food you should not eat too much of.

You can get a copy of the food guide showing the pyramid shape by writing Room 344, Human Nutrition Information Service, 6505 Belcrest Road, Hyattsville, Md. 20782.

If a mosquito bites someone with AIDS and bites someone else, will that second person get AIDS?

Veronica Shackleford, Detroit

No. Mosquitoes do not spread the virus that causes AIDS — acquired immunodeficiency syndrome.

AIDS is a human disease, not one mosquitoes have or carry.

People who study AIDS have done tests on mosquitoes. In the tests, scientists exposed mosquitoes to infected blood to see whether they spread the virus. They didn't.

In other studies, scientists looked at areas in the world where there are a lot of people with AIDS and a lot of mosquitoes. Doctors always were able to find a specific cause, not mosquitoes, for each case of AIDS.

In those places, no one ever got AIDS except in cases involving sexual contact without protection, using dirty needles to take drugs or an infected mother passing it on to a newborn.

Some mosquitoes carry germs or viruses of other diseases. But mosquitoes don't leave blood. They suck it when they bite. The germs for a few diseases, such as malaria, are spread through the spit-like substances mosquitoes leave when they suck the blood out. That isn't true with AIDS.

What does AIDS do to the body? What parts of the body does AIDS affect?

Michael Simon, Birmingham

Many parts of the body are affected.

That's because the most common problem for people with the disease is a weakened immune system and loss of white blood cells. These are cells that can be seen only through a microscope. Loss of these cells makes it hard for the body to fight off germs that cause infections. A weak immune system also makes it easier for cancers or tumors to develop.

The parts of the body where infections, cancers or other types of direct damage from viruses are most common are the skin, the lungs, the brain and the nerves that get messages from the brain for the rest of the body, the eyes, the stomach and the intestines.

Other diseases that are often more common are called opportunistic — meaning they can't usually enter the body unless its immune system is weak. These include certain cancers and tumors. They can happen in almost any part of the body.

Two of the more common cancers someone with AIDS may have are:

■ Lymphoma (lim-FOH-muh), a type of cancer that leads to tumors in the brain and other parts of the body;

■ Kaposi's (KAP-oh-seez) sarcoma (sar-KOH-muh), a type of cancer that usually grows in the skin, but also in the body. It can begin as soft, raised, purplish bumps.

A common infection is pneumocystis (new-mo-SIS-tiss) carinii (car-IN-nee) pneumonia (new-MOAN-yuh). This affects the lungs, irritating them so it becomes difficult to get oxygen needed for the body.

108

Most of these infections can be treated, but eventually infections or cancers take over the immune systems of many people with AIDS, and the body can't fight them anymore.

What is the difference between HIV-positive and AIDS?

Tiffany Williams, Detroit

"HIV-positive" refers to a person who has the human immunodeficiency virus in his or her body. (The person is said to have "tested positive" for the virus.)

Having AIDS means a person has the virus in his or her body and also has other problems or diseases because he or she has a weakened immune system.

Generally, people are said to have AIDS when their immune systems can't fight off certain types of infections that are called opportunistic (op-er-too-NISS-tick) infections. They are called opportunistic because the virus has given these germs a chance, or opportunity, to enter the body and make the person sick. A healthy immune system can prevent these types of infections.

It takes an average of 10 years to develop AIDS after being infected by HIV. HIV weakens the body's defense systems gradually, and a person who has HIV can be healthy for a long time.

Will they ever discover a shot for AIDS?

Jessica Solomon, Grosse Pointe Woods

Probably — but it will probably take several years to get a shot that prevents AIDS.

There are medicines and treatments that keep the virus that causes AIDS from growing quickly in the body. There also are improvements in the drugs to treat the infections that people with AIDS often have.

For prevention, doctors and researchers have been testing some types of vaccine (vack-SEEN), similar to what children get before starting school to prevent measles, polio and other serious diseases.

There are some vaccines now being tested in monkeys, but no vaccine tests have been done on people to see whether the vaccines prevent AIDS.

Setting up tests on people takes time and must have an OK from the countries where people would be tested.

Once the vaccine is tested on people, it probably would take several years to know whether it really worked.

Many people, including some at the University of Michigan in Ann Arbor, are working to find a vaccine.

Could AIDS be transmitted by ear-piercing?

Katie Turnbull, Grosse Pointe

The virus that can lead to AIDS is called HIV — which stands for human immunodeficiency virus. It can be transmitted by ear-piercing when a needle is shared.

If the needle used to pierce a person's ear has blood on it, and if that blood carries HIV, the virus can enter the ear tissue or bloodstream.

Other blood infections also can be passed through shared needles used in ear-piercing.

Most doctors recommend that people not try to pierce ears at home, because most people don't have the right materials to get a needle free of germs.

They suggest going to a doctor for ear-piercing, or to a place where it's certain the needle or instrument used to pierce the ears will be free of germs.

The problem is in sharing needles. If another method is used — such as piercing the ear with an unused earring — and that instrument isn't shared, there is not the same risk.

How come people with AIDS lose their hair?

Leika Raychouni, Dearborn

Here are three main reasons:

■ The first is part of the disease's name — the "D" for "deficiency." In an AIDS patient, the body's system for fighting off disease is weak, or deficient.

That means AIDS patients come down with illnesses that other people would be able to fight off. In advanced cases, many AIDS patients develop various kinds of cancer.

Doctors end up treating them with strong anticancer drugs, which act on parts of the body that are growing rapidly. The drugs may destroy fast-growing lumps of cancer, called tumors. They also may destroy other fast-growing parts of the body, including hair.

■ A second reason AIDS patients may lose their hair is that those in late stages of AIDS often suffer from what is called wasting syndrome. People with wasting syndrome often lose their appetites and may suffer from diarrhea (die-uh-REE-uh), which keeps their bodies from absorbing food well. The nutrients in food are what keep hair growing. Lack of nutrients can cause loss of hair, muscle tissue and body weight.

■ A third reason is that some people with AIDS also have a sexually transmitted disease called syphilis (SIF-fill-iss). A symptom of syphilis is hair loss.

Doctors are still studying the effects of AIDS. They don't yet know all the reasons for hair loss in patients.

By Bill Laitner

Holidays

Why is Thanksgiving on a Thursday; why not on a Monday or a Tuesday?

Wyaudtnoong Adams, Traverse City

The Thursday tradition goes back to the late 1600s, long before President Abraham Lincoln made the last Thursday in November an official national holiday.

When pioneers in Massachusetts celebrated a day of thanks, they didn't want a day that would be close to Sunday.

That left Tuesday through Thursday. Because Thursday was often a day of prayer and lectures or sermons by Puritan ministers, making that a day of thanks would build on a weekly habit. At the time, Thanksgiving was mainly a day of reflection and prayer.

By 1863, when President Lincoln made it a national holiday (which a female writer and editor, Sarah Hale, suggested and campaigned for), an autumn Thursday for a day of thanks and a day off work already was a tradition in many states.

113

How did Groundhog Day begin?

Amber Lee Adamick, Livonia

The American celebration of this day goes back mainly to German settlers who watched animals for signs of spring.

Germans watched for a hibernating animal — one whose body's systems had slowed down for the winter — to appear. If this

animal, such as a badger or a bear, came out and saw sunshine, it supposedly would be frightened by the shadows and go back to sleep. That would mean 40 more days of winter.

When people came to America, there were not as many badgers or bears to watch, so people watched another hibernating animal, the groundhog, for weather predictions. The common belief here, too, was that if the day were sunny, the groundhog would see its shadow and go back underground. That would mean six more weeks of winter. Weather experts have never found that this method of predicting really works.

Which holiday celebration-wise is more dangerous, Memorial Day or the Fourth of July?

Anthony Byrd, Detroit

The Fourth of July is generally when there are more accidents or deaths.

It's one of the most dangerous holidays for these reasons:

■ Lots of people are out driving, and some of the drivers have been drinking alcohol, so there are generally more traffic deaths than on Memorial Day. (Labor Day in September, though, generally has more than the Fourth of July.)

■ The activities in July — boating, swimming and fireworks — bring more dangers. There are more drownings in July than May. For example, of the more than 12,000 fireworks-related accidents each year in the United States, two-thirds happen in July. More than one-third of the fireworks injuries happen to people 14 and younger.

Here are some tips:

■ No children should use fireworks, legal or illegal.
■ Buckle your seat belt when you're in a car.
■ Wear a life jacket at all times in a boat.

Why are there fireworks on the Fourth of July?

Aisha Graham, Detroit

Fireworks are used, in part, because that's what one of the early leaders of this country, John Adams, suggested in 1776.

He wrote to his wife that the separation from England deserved to be celebrated with parades and fireworks. He suggested July 2. But the official vote to become an independent country wasn't until July 4, which became the holiday.

Using fireworks for important events was already common in America. Settlers brought the custom from England. It was a way royalty had to mark any special event.

The Americans took that British tradition and used fireworks, along with firing cannons and guns, as a way to mark the holiday.

Fireworks displays, though, may go back to the Chinese people more than 1,000 years ago. About 600 years ago, soldiers fighting in Asia brought them to Europe.

More fireworks are set off for the Fourth of July than for any other national celebration in the world

How was Devil's Night started?

Jenee Rowe, Suttons Bay

The idea of tricks around Halloween is more than 2,000 years old. Tricks became part of the tradition, especially in Ireland, because Halloween was when the new year started. A new year meant time to say good-bye to spirits and to ancestors that had died. It also meant people needed to protect themselves from spirits who visited

Earth on that day.

Making fires was part of the tradition. A bonfire honored the sun for a good harvest and frightened away spirits.

This tradition came to America in the middle to late 1800s, when lots of Irish people came to America.

In Boston at the time, an Irish Halloween custom of setting bonfires was discouraged because it was dangerous when flames spread into buildings. The Irish tradition also involved tricks and pranks.

To discourage tricks, adults tried to encourage another custom — giving treats. Children wanted to do both. Some kept the custom of bonfires but did it on the day before Halloween; they still got treats on Halloween.

Irish immigrants may also have brought the customs to Detroit and to Michigan. "Devil's Night" became a night for tricks as early as the 1920s. Sometimes it was even called "Mischief Night" or "Cabbage Night" because people would throw cabbages or put cabbages on their porches.

By the 1960s, the pranks sometimes became more harmful. Old newspapers show that young people occasionally broke windows in schools and cars. Another huge problem was false fire alarms.

By the early 1980s, Devil's Night had become known for fires. Abandoned homes and buildings were a problem, and people set fires in them. Sometimes the fires would spread to houses where people lived.

The year 1984 was the worst, with 297 fires reported on Devil's Night. Since then, the City of Detroit has organized volunteers to help the police on Devil's Night, and fires have become less of a problem.

By Bill McGraw and Cathy Collison

Just curious

How big are the Oscars? How much are they worth?

Kate Roginski, Wyandotte

The Oscar statue given to Academy Award winners is 13 1/2 inches tall and weighs 8 pounds.

It is made by R.S. Owens & Co. of Chicago. It is made of Britannia metal coated in gold. The company is not allowed to tell its value.

The Oscar statue has always had some gold on it except during World War II, when is was made of plaster.

Who designed the first Barbie doll?

Andrienne Lesperance, Lincoln Park

A team of people designed the first Barbie doll, which came out in 1959.

But one person, Ruth Handler, came up with the idea of Barbie and supervised the making of the doll at the toy company, Mattel Inc.

Handler had seen her own daughter Barbara have a lot of fun with paper dolls. The paper dolls her daughter chose were always the grown-up ones.

Handler saw that her daughter liked to use the dolls and pretend to dress them in adult fashions.

She decided she wanted to make a real doll like the paper dolls. When traveling in Switzerland, she saw a doll that came close. She bought one for her daughter. But that doll was sold with only one outfit.

Back home, she started work on an American doll that would have different outfits. The first Barbie was shown at a toy fair in 1959.

When did the Army get white uniforms?

Monica Olmsted, Monroe

The Army has had white uniforms for more than 100 years, but you don't see them very often in the United States. They are just for special occasions. In the United States, soldiers and officers can wear so-called dress whites only in the warm weather between April and October. In warm climates, they can wear them year-round.

In colder weather here, soldiers wear blue wool uniforms, called dress blues, for special occasions. Because they have to buy the dress uniforms themselves, many don't get both a blue one and a white one.

The white uniforms, made of either cotton or polyester blends, are cooler in the summer.

White caps come with the uniform. For top officers, at the rank of major or above, the white cap has two arcs of oak leaves embroidered on it. An officer's sleeve is also different on the white uniform. Officers have a mohair braid on each sleeve.

Why do people float in space?

Danny Luce, Bay City

People don't really float in space.

They're falling, but they're going so fast sideways that the motion offsets the effect of the Earth's gravity, which is the force that pulls objects to the Earth.

It works only if they are going the right speed — about 17,000 miles an hour. That's called orbital speed — the speed needed for an object to keep going around the Earth. If the speed is slower, astronauts, shuttles and satellites would begin to fall back to Earth. If a shuttle or a satellite went faster, it would go out of the Earth's orbit into space instead of circling.

The floating effect in space is really weightlessness, because astronauts don't feel any weight. Astronauts say they feel more like they are falling than like they're floating, as you would on water when you swim.

When you're on Earth, you feel your weight when you're standing on the ground. If the ground — or a floor — were taken out from underneath you, you would not feel the weight and would fall.

How come people remember so clearly exactly what they were doing when Pearl Harbor got bombed and when John Fitzgerald Kennedy was shot?

Abe Lorber, Huntington Woods

The reason is that the people had powerful feelings when they heard of those events. Anger, sadness and perhaps fear were some of the feelings people had when they heard about President John F. Kennedy being shot on Nov. 22, 1963, or Pearl Harbor being bombed on Dec. 7, 1941.

When events lead to strong feelings — such as anger or fear — a part of the brain called the hippocampus (hip-uh-CAM-pus) combines the messages from the feelings with messages from the other senses (what a person saw, heard or even tasted).

People sometimes call that type of memory a "flashbulb memory" — because it is as if the mind takes a picture at that time and records the images of almost everything that the person was doing.

The brain records all memories, but that type of memory stands out.

Why is a barn red?

John Bergeron, Sault Ste. Marie

A lot of barns have been painted red because red paint doesn't cost much and is easy to make.

That's because the paint is made of oil mixed with rust, iron oxide, which is found in rocks and dirt. The rust gives the paint its red color.

Farmers used to make paint, usually buying iron oxide and adding the oil themselves.

But new barns are more likely to be made of metal, not wood, that is painted at the factory. Their color is often white; but green, blue and gray are popular, too. These barns can cost less than building a wood barn that would have to be painted.

The new metal barns also are more popular with farmers because the metal barns have fewer openings for wind, rain and snow to get in. That keeps animals that live in the barn healthier. Metal barns are also easier to clean.

You will see fewer red barns in the next couple of years as more farmers buy metal barns.

Why do weird things happen in the Bermuda Triangle?

Sarah Chase, Riverview

Disasters there are not really unusual to groups such as the U.S. Coast Guard, which patrols those waters.

Recently, some people thought they found traces of five Navy planes that vanished together in 1945, but it turned out to be pieces of other planes.

The Coast Guard says ships and planes vanish in this area for two main reasons: human error, in which a person made a mistake, and natural factors.

Natural factors include:

■ A fast ocean current, the Gulf Stream, which takes wreckage and spreads it out quickly.

■ Very changeable weather. Storms start quickly, creating large waves and waterspouts — water rising like a tornado that can pull a plane down.

■ Ditches — some more than a mile deep — in the ocean floor.

What do the "a.m." and "p.m." stand for in time?

Lindsay Abbott, Farmington Hills

"A.M." stands for "ante" (AN-tee) "meridiem" (muh-RIDD-ee-um). "P.M." stands for "post meridiem" (muh-RIDD-ee-um). Those words are Latin. "Ante meridiem" means "before noon" and "post meridiem" means "after noon."

What does the expression "Indian giver" mean?

David Gault, St. Clair Shores

It means giving something as a gift, then taking it back. It's an insult to the person who gets called an "Indian giver." It also is an insult to American Indians.

The words were never used by Indians. Settlers and white Americans used them more than 150 years ago.

Some white Americans long ago believed it was a custom for American Indians to take back gifts if they didn't get equally valuable ones in return. This was a big misunderstanding.

Native American cultures do not permit people ever to take a gift back. Usually, when a gift is given, that person or someone else in the family will get a gift or favor in return at some time.

By the way, nowadays, "Indian giver" is also sometimes used to describe the American settlers who kept giving the Indians land to live on, then taking it back and giving them worse land in return. From the Indian perspective, "European-giver" could be the more accurate term.

I was wondering how salt melts snow and ice. Please tell me.

Maria Szawronskyj, Sterling Heights

Salt melts snow and ice by changing the freezing point of water.

Water freezes at 32 degrees Fahrenheit. But when salt is added, the salt crystals dissolve into the ice, creating a mixture called brine, which is part salt and part water. Brine has a much lower freezing point, about minus 6 degrees, depending on how much salt is in the water.

The temperature affects how much salt is needed to melt snow and ice. The lower the temperature, the more salt is needed and the longer it takes. For example, at 30 degrees, a pound of salt would melt 46.3 pounds of ice; but at 10 degrees, 1 pound of salt would melt only about 5 pounds of ice.

Besides melting the ice, salt breaks up the bond between the ice and the pavement. The more this is broken, the easier it is for snowplows to finish the job of clearing the roads.

In some big snowtorms, road crews in Wayne County, which includes Detroit, have used 20,000 tons of salt — that's enough to cover a football field in 10 feet of salt.

Acknowledgments

This book never would have come to be if it weren't for the editors and writers who first conceived of News for Young Readers in 1991 and then made it a regular Detroit Free Press feature — and who continue to give it their full support. Among them are Marty Claus, Ann Olson, Deborah Withey, Chip Visci, Heath Meriwether, Amy Wilson and Dale Parry. Others who are never too busy to answer this writer's questions include Chuck Mitchell, Ron Dzwonkowski, Dave Robinson, Owen Davis, Michelle Kaufman, Gene Myers, Bill McGraw and the Detroit Free Press reporting and library staff.

Making things clear for young readers means every answer you see had at least four — sometimes more — reads. Those with a special eye for clarity are Barbara Arrigo, Kathy Warbelow, Alex Cruden and the copy editors who work with them.

Reporting for young readers means reading books, magazines and newspapers for background as well as talking to experts close to home and around the country.

These are among the many people, organizations and materials that have helped answer young readers' questions:

Detroit Free Press library, staff writers and editors.

Professors, associates and others from the University of Michigan, especially Richard Bailey, Roy Clarke, Terry Gallagher, George Grassmuck, Michael Hayes, Ted Hopf, Robert Payne, Kim Lane Scheppele, Peter Sousounis, Rob Van der Voo, Peter Van Minnen, Martin Walsh and Myron Wegman; from Michigan State University, especially David Batch, Dr. Dave Roberts and Thomas Vogel; from Wayne State University, especially Dr. Patti Brown, Rob Butler and Janet Langlois; and from Central Michigan University, especially Dr. Wayne Kiefer.

Other experts, including Albert Bartley, University of Colorado; Paul Boller, Texas Christian University; Mark Bonito, U.S. Geological Survey-Menlo Park in California; Bob Cosgrove, Indian Village Historical Collections; Gary Dunn, Young Entomologists Society; Rayna Green, American Indian Program at the Smithsonian Institution; James Harding, Michigan State University Museum; Jim Henderson, National Severe Storms Forecast Center; Elise Horeath, Environmental Protection Agency; Dave Huxhold, Akzo Salt; Joan LaBine, Oakland County Health Department; Roy Laishley, African Recovery, a United Nations news service; Dr. Chris Lewandowski, Henry Ford Hospital; Wayne Maley, American Society of Agricultural Engineers; Dr. Joseph Mendels, Memory Institute of Philadelphia; Dr. Alvin Michaels of Bingham Farms; Dr. Ellen Moore, Children's Hospital of Michigan; Jerrie Nichols, U.S. Fish and Wildlife Service;

Karen Nuytten, Saratoga Community Hospital in Detroit; Dr. Michele Nypaver, Henry Ford Hospital; Fred Piper, Michigan Department of Transportation; Randy Pope, Michigan Department of Public Health; Susan Pyle, American Red Cross; Dr. Karl Seifert, Iowa State University; Jimmy Schmidt; Jim Sharp, National Air and Space Museum's Albert Einstein Planetarium; Joel Smith, Environmental Protection Agency; Peggy Timlin, Pilgrim Society in Plymouth, Mass.; Gerry Van Lew, Michigan Department of Transportation; Stephen Wayne, Georgetown University; Brad Wittman, Michigan Secretary of State's Bureau of Elections; Dr. Kathryn Wright, HIV/adolescent clinic at Detroit Medical Center.

Organizations, including AAA Michigan; the American Pyrotechnics Association; Baseball Hall of Fame; Cranbrook Institute of Science; Detroit Zoo; Major League Umpires Association; Michigan State University's Abrams Planetarium; National Weather Service; National Safety Council; National Severe Storm Center; the Safety Council for Southeastern Michigan; U.S. Army Corps of Engineers; U.S. House of Representatives parliamentarian's staff; University of Minnesota's Center for Ancient Times; Wellness Networks Inc.; the White House staff.

Many books, periodicals and newspapers exploring specific areas:
"The Complete Book of the Olympics"
Detroit Free Press wire services and Knight-Ridder newspapers
"Dictionary of Word Origins"
"Encyclopedia of Word and Phrase Origins"
"The Life of Birds" by Joel Welty
"The Olympics Factbook"
"The President: Tidbits and Trivia"
Science magazine
"Snowflakes" by Joan Sugarman
"This Restless Earth" (Random House)
"Volcanoes in Action" (McGraw-Hill)
"Weather" (Time-Life Books)
The World Almanac
The World Book Encyclopedia
The World Book Medical Encyclopedia